Dissenter in a Great Society

Dissenter in a Great Society

A Christian View of America in Crisis

William Stringfellow

ABINGDON
PRESS
NASHVILLE
NEW YORK

PRINTED AND BOUND BY THE PARTHENON PRESS, AT
NASHVILLE, TENNESSEE, UNITED STATES OF AMERICA

For Mr. Blue

FOREWORD   This book originates in my own practical involvement as a Christian who is a citizen of the United States. It represents spontaneous reactions to certain contemporary happenings, sometimes in indignation, sometimes in grief, in frustration, in hope, in depression, sometimes—I suppose—in idealism, sometimes in apprehension, sometimes in anguish. These are reflections on American society from the peculiar vantage of a Christian. While they furnish no predictions, they are weighed heavily with the premonition that this nation is engaged in suicide and that its self-destruction is being pursued in the name of supposedly admirable purposes: nationalism, survival, domestic tranquillity, resistance to aggression or aid to the development of other countries, the maturing of democracy, the construction of a great society.

These are theological comments, not social criticism or political analyses, although biblically it is impossible to separate theology from these other matters. These essays make no pretense to being either wholly consistent or utterly coherent; they embody an attempt to respond in terms of the versatility of Christ's Gospel to particular aspects of the American social crisis, especially as it has been manifest since 1964.

This book has no other ambition than to be a chronicle of criticism, complaint, and dissent, informed, I trust, by the faith and ministry exemplified in Christ, in which all things whatsoever are brought into question in this life.

Appreciation belongs to Catherine Oleson, Joseph Cunneen, Anthony Towne, and Peter Rooney for help in readying the manuscript.

Some material here was first presented in lectures and articles, including those at the Harvard Law School, the Michigan Judicial Conference, the American Orthopsychiatric Association Convention, Immaculate Heart College, Emory University, Union Theological Seminary in New York, the Episcopal House of Bishops, the 1965 Roman Catholic Liturgical Conference, the Australian Council of Churches, and in *Law and Contemporary Social Problems, Motive, The Christian Cen-*

tury, The Notre Dame Lawyer, Ramparts, Presbyterian Survey, and *Katallegate.*

Except for the New English Bible citation introducing the final chapter, biblical quotations are from the *Revised Standard Version of the Bible,* copyrighted 1946 and 1952 by the Division of Christian Education, National Council of Churches and used by permission.

WILLIAM STRINGFELLOW

Rogation Sunday, 1966
New York City

Chapter One

Poverty, Property, and People

I do not mean that others should be eased and you burdened, but that as a matter of equality your abundance at the present time should supply their want, so that their abundance may supply your want, that there may be equality.

II Corinthians 8:13–14

AMERICA has the technical capacity to abolish poverty; the question is: does it have the moral capability to do so?

Poverty is a paradox in America because we have the means to banish poverty. This nation has the natural and synthetic resources, productive potential, economic incentive, technological sophistication, and ideological rationale requisite to house, clothe, feed, educate, employ, and admit to political responsibility all its citizens. Yet poverty persists.

In this respect the United States differs from certain other nations beset by poverty. Haiti, for instance, is possessed of neither the technical capability nor the moral commitment to free her people from the poverty that enslaves them. In India, although conscience has been aroused on behalf of the multitudes of her poor, there does not yet exist either the economic stability or the industrial development needed to overcome poverty. But in the United States poverty is not a matter of the absence or underdevelopment of resources or of the skills to harness those resources: here the issue is whether well-established institutions and prosperous citizens are mature enough in a moral sense to be committed to the abolition of poverty.

What accounts morally for the persistence of poverty in America? Negligence, apathy, corruption, stupidity, myopia, greed—or, most likely, all these tangled together. Whatever the case, in the midst of such incomparable affluence, not to say bizarre extravagance, poverty in the United States undermines the credibility of the American idea of society among Americans who are poor, challenges the ethics of democracy, and tarnishes the image of this country throughout the world.

Poverty in America does not mean—as it still does in so many other lands—mud huts, residual feudalism,

3

nakedness, starvation, and epidemic. Here it means millions of citizens imprisoned in squalid urban ghettos and in tar-paper shacks in the hinterlands, chronic unemployment, the specter of permanent unemployability, and seeing one's children embark for the same dead ends by being consigned to decrepit, ill-equipped, overcrowded, and understaffed schools. It means the stifling of initiative of countless citizens unable to obtain a small-business loan, home mortgage, or other form of conventional credit because of racial discrimination. It means surrender of family privacy and personal dignity to satisfy the bureaucratic requirements of welfare investigators.

While most Americans have occasional generous twinges and dutifully support the conventional charities, by and large they have no exposure to the actual experience of the poor. It is hard for them to realize that there are fellow Americans today who are still being denied the right of suffrage by intimidation, fraud, and mayhem; who are suffering the condescensions of the prosperous in order to get and keep servile jobs; who are enduring the importunities of slumlords, loan sharks, and clubhouse politicians who profiteer off the poor, and who are always being admonished to patiently wait for a better day—which is virtually certain not to come if awaited patiently. Poverty in America is to be unwelcome, unwanted, and apparently unneeded in the society of one's own citizenship and birthright. It means the despair of any human hope that something will happen in the discernible future that might significantly change the day-to-day existence of those men, women, and children who are poor.

A War Against the Poor?

True, a war on poverty has been declared, but, as of now, it seems more an appeasement of the conscience of the prosperous than empathy for the sufferings of the poor.

The war on poverty is, of course, still in its infancy and there are no reasons to have expected overnight remedies for the deep-seated inequities in education and employment opportunities, associated as these usually are with racism and ghettoization. There is, moreover, a serious prospect that the effort will be scuttled altogether if the American foreign military involvements continue to expand. Yet, taking such considerations into account, and assuming the sincere intentions of those charged with prosecution of the war on poverty in the national administration, the fact remains that the effort is grossly disproportionate to the needs of the poor and the whole of society. Poverty cannot be undone in America by appropriating a nickel where five dollars is required.

The impoverishment of the war on poverty, the comparatively meager funds designated for antipoverty programs, means that at best they are addressed to symptoms rather than to causes, and lack the fundamental insight that the continuation of poverty in a rich nation like the United States is a sign of moral decadence.

I have no sympathy for the short-sighted who oppose the war on poverty and do not even recognize their own self-interest in overcoming the huge depletion in the gross national product for which poverty accounts (more than five billions of dollars in 1964 alone). I mean to provide no pretexts for further evasions by those who are so enamored of greed that they denounce any assistance to the poor at all. I do not countenance the cynics who are so bereft of compassion for human suffering that they excuse their own indifference by blaming poverty upon the poor. Nevertheless, the self-indulgence of the myopic, the greedy, and the cynical does not save the present war on poverty from criticism. In fact, it makes responsible scrutiny of all present programs—national, state, and city—all the more necessary and relevant.

Fundamentally, the war on poverty, as it is now conceived and as it is now being pursued, is most unlikely to reap the kind of social change essential to the abolition of poverty, because it does not attack the institutionalization of poverty in America. More specifically, it is too often a mere extension of the traditional welfare concept in which people entrapped in poverty are provided the bare essentials of survival in food and clothing and shelter and medical care but do not acquire skills and jobs which would enable them to provide in these ways for themselves. In the summer of 1965, for example, several thousand Harlem adolescents, mostly from deprived educational backgrounds, without marketable job qualifications, were provided summer employment in temporary, marginal, unskilled jobs. No doubt these occupations helped to relieve the tensions of the summer months for these youths. Perhaps these stop-gap jobs helped avert riot. But that season has ended and the same kids are again unemployed and remain unemployable. The summer jobs did not lead to permanent ones or to the acquisition of occupational skills. At the most, this program was a form of charity, necessary maybe in an urgent situation but of no serious consequence in lifting these adolescents out

of poverty by remedial education or job training. The
expansion of charity, while it may provide some children
with milk, or pay the rent on a slum tenement, or divert
unemployable school dropouts for a couple of months,
opens no exits from poverty.

Poverty and Social Change

Meanwhile, there are societies on the face of the globe
where poverty has been radically diminished, notably in
Western Europe since the end of the Second World War.
In America the times are considered secure and healthy
if unemployment is computed at the level of three or four
per cent. In Britain, despite the erosion of its wealth due
to the contraction of empire, less than one-tenth of one
per cent are unemployed at the same time. One remedy
on which the British have relied in virtually abolishing
unemployment in the face of automation and cybernation
is, of course, "made work." Jobs are created and multiplied
for the sake of making employment, on the principle that
it is more human for people to be occupied in work than
to be idle, and more economical for people to be employed—and thus become consumers and taxpayers—
than to be the mere recipients of charity, either public or
private. I realize that "made work" seems alien to many
Americans and that it is especially objectionable, in theory
anyway, to white Anglo-Saxon Protestant Americans who
regard work as a virtue only if it is tangibly productive.
Ironically, in the United States the phenomenon of "made
work" has become very common indeed among the middle
classes of mainly white, college-educated citizens who find
employment in pseudoprofessional "service" positions

which, according to a strictly conservative laissez-faire
doctrine, could and should be eliminated. Increasingly,
college graduates end up as mere middlemen—salesmen,
factors, brokers, consultants, agents, insurers, administrative assistants, promoters, and the like. If these forms of
"made work" are an appropriate prospect for the white
bourgeoisie, let the same principle as in some other societies become applicable in America for the poor.

As the impact of automation has become more visible
and the fantastic potential of cybernation has begun to be
more widely understood, some proposals for the conserva-
tion of existing jobs have been advanced, as well as some
ideas for the creation of additional jobs in surviving trades
and occupations. The railroad brotherhoods have fought
in contract negotiations to secure guarantees that certain
jobs would be maintained even after machines have replaced men in doing the work. This must be counted as a
negative approach toward automation which, at the most,
delays automation for a relatively brief time—until those
whose jobs are so secured reach retirement age. Although
a reactionary response to technological change, it does
have the commendable objective of keeping men employed who, if abruptly displaced by mechanization,
would become unemployable because their now obsolete
skills are the only ones they possess and they are too old
for retraining. Still, much more imaginative steps than
this freezing of present employment must be undertaken,
both publicly and privately, if cybernation and automation are to become humanly beneficial rather than a
Frankenstein in this society.

A modest beginning would be the reduction of the
work week, thereby both preserving existing jobs and
multiplying hirings. It is no panacea, but the shortening

of the work week without a corresponding reduction in wages, if accompanied by safeguards against "moonlighting" (where one man holds two jobs instead of two men each having a job), could significantly increase employment.

Would such "new" jobs, created by a briefer work week, actually become available to those who are poor and now unemployed or those who are not now hired because of racial barriers in unionization and employer practices? I suspect not, as things are now. The unions in very many industries and trades would have to become seriously democratized and integrated, so far as eligibility for union membership is concerned; recruitment and employment procedures of business would have to be revamped, especially with respect to racial practices; and, most important of all, if a shortened work week is to be a means of increasing employment to alleviate poverty, both labor and management would have to provide far more on-the-job training facilities to fill the additional jobs made in this way.

Moreover, an abbreviated work week holds promise of creating employment in areas where little prior experience or technical preparation are required. If the work week is cut from forty to, say, twenty-five hours, there would surely be a further expansion of the so-called leisure industries. There would be more bowling alleys and more bars, more highways and more motels, more billboards and promotions, more fads and phoniness, more tourists and more novelties for them to purchase, more sights for them to see, more clothes for them to affect, more dietary beverages for them to gulp, more refuse to pick up after them—more of everything that seems tawdry in American leisure. It is, in one sense, a vulgar prospect in which so much that is offensive and prodigal about America would be proliferated deliberately. And all the while there will also be more traffic accidents, more loitering, more boredom, more superficiality, more loneliness, more suicide, and more evidences of decadence and death instead of life.

But that is only part of the prospect *if* poverty is to be alleviated by employment. A short work week which drastically expands the so-called leisure industries would, in very many instances, create jobs for which skills requiring prolonged or extensive qualification are not required. The irony of automation, it seems to me, which has not yet been enough appreciated, is that by contracting and consolidating the productive apparatus in tangible goods, there can be an enormous multiplication and diversification in occupations and trades not dependent upon highly sophisticated education. Automation, a symbol and synonym of the displacement of human skills, offers the possibility, if Americans are not paralyzed in coping with it, of a tremendous increase in technically unskilled occupations which service the new leisure of men and, with any sort of luck, offers also an exciting and broad escalation of creative and performing arts. Yes, there would be more commercialism and more Coke, more brothels and more booze. By exactly the same token, by just the same human possibility, however, there can be jobs and leisure for practically everybody and the occasion and opportunity to use the rewards of work for a leisure which is edifying and maturing.

In such an era, therefore, there could be more parades, more dancing, more painting and more poetry, more opera, more ballet, more creativity and more literacy, more beauty and more occasions to savor the beautiful or, at least, consider what beauty is, more music and more singing, more circuses of course, more kite flying, more honest self-expression, more human play, more exuberance in the gift of life, and, maybe, even more time for love and those few things that are really important.

That carries us far beyond the relatively simple device of shortening the work week, I realize. It implies that this society finally recognize that to read or write or paint or perform in a creative and original way or to conscientiously study such matters is an honest, respectable, and socially significant form of work which, as the Bible says, is worthy of hire and has as good a claim on just compensation as the work of merchants, manufacturers, managers, farmers, lenders, brokers, governors, and thieves.

As an initial example of socially useful work entitled to compensation, I would advocate the payment of wage stipends to university students. While public subsidies and private philanthropies have, in the past decade or so, significantly expanded access to higher education in America, in most instances the chief admissions credential for college or graduate work is the ability to pay the costs of such education. This has meant that university education has remained class-oriented in this country, at the very time that a college degree has become more determinative of employment prospects. What must be done, however, is to remove the economic barrier to higher education and make it available to students, as far as possible, on the basis of sheer academic and intellectual qualification and potential. And let it be recognized that some persons qualified to be students, because of the inherited inequities in American society, bear burdens which are not lifted by the extension of credit for tuition fees or student loans or openings for student employment. Let study itself be acknowledged as socially utilitarian, so that a student will receive not only tuition and room and board, but a salary for doing his work, thus enabling him, while a student, to maintain his family and meet his basic personal responsibilities.

If study were recognized and compensated for as (what it is in fact) work, not only would the class qualification for admission to higher education be seriously modified, but the academic standards for admissions would be powerfully strengthened. Incidentally, I suspect that America would begin to have a few colleges and universities which would be significantly integrated. More people of all sorts would become employable, and it would mean something, apart from social status, to be a college graduate. In this way our society might take a step toward recognizing that among the varieties of work which have social importance are the activities of creative intelligence. If we begin to acknowledge study as work, there is a chance that creativity will also, finally, become an employable skill in this society.

If something like that ever happened, I believe there would be a surplus of jobs. That could be the day poverty would be abolished.

The Politics of Poverty

There has been much talk about a war on poverty, but that war has been woefully underfinanced, and up to now its program has been largely an extension of outmoded welfare remedies. If it is not yet basically geared to the creation of employment, if social attitudes among the prosperous have not yet accepted the multiplication of jobs as a means of eliminating poverty, if so far it represents a dilettante concern for the poor, with all the paternalism which that implies, it nevertheless has some things to its credit already: it has opened a new pork barrel for local politicians; it is a bonanza in both new positions and greater prestige for the social work bureaucracy; it is a sop for the conscience of the affluent, and it has devised some ways of distracting the attention of the poor from their distress. If, in the process, some school dropouts are finally taught to read and write, or some birth control information is disseminated, or some women learn how to keep house, then so much the dividend.

Ever since poverty became a major societal issue, both parties have been playing politics with the Devil. The titular leader of one party has repeatedly expressed contempt for the poor, while the incumbent national administration has so far evinced little more than a ceremonial concern for the stubborn and harsh realities of poverty in American society. To the numberless men of integrity, talent, and enterprise who suffer emasculation because they were born black, who are wasted because they have been educationally deprived, who are restricted to marginal and menial jobs and now face the prospect that even these become obsolete and eliminated, Barry Goldwater speaks fondly of individual initiative. President Johnson prosecutes the war on poverty by repackaging existing programs and obsolete ideas, uttering pronouncements, issuing press releases, and requesting meager appropriations. As far as poverty is concerned, the choice is between nihilists and nominalists. Meanwhile, millions of people are born, endure for a while, and then die, all the while prisoners of the urban ghettos or the rural wastelands.

For the lesser politicians, the war on poverty is almost universally looked upon as patronage to be deployed where it will most likely entrench or enhance incumbent powers. That is precisely the reason why in most cities— Philadelphia is an exception, San Francisco is struggling to become one—no provision has been made or even seriously contemplated for the representation of the poor themselves in the administration of poverty programs, although it is specifically authorized by law. That is also why two high officials—William Haddad and Adam Yarmolinsky—who sought to activate that provision of the law, were eased out of their positions in the war on poverty. Significantly, regional and partisan differences had little significance in the pressures that brought about the departures of these two experienced, dedicated, and able men. Yarmolinsky's resignation was a price exacted from the President for support of poverty appropriations by Southern conservatives who feared that if Yarmolinsky had his way, he might prevent poverty patronage from benefiting segregationists. Haddad was sacrificed because several New York City congressmen—professed liberals to a man—feared that his insistence on representation of the poor might make him politically popular with the poor, and perhaps before long he might unseat one of them. In Chicago, where Mayor Daley stands for massive resistance to the representation of the poor, it takes no genius to figure out that Daley is partly motivated by apprehensions about the political future in Illinois of Sargent Shriver.

The local politicians have reason to be worried: if the poor were genuinely represented, and indigenous com-

munity organizations of the poor developed, the poor
would begin to mature as a new political power, they
would have a chance to be freed from dependence upon
doles, and a new political alignment would emerge that
would certainly diminish—and probably, sooner or later,
overthrow—the existing political leaders in many localities, particularly in the larger cities.

All kinds of rationalizations can be summoned to deny
the poor representation in running the war on poverty.
The poor have no experience in administration—yes, but
how will they ever obtain such experience except in the
development of just the sort of community organizations
which the policy of the poverty legislation envisions? The
poor would make mistakes—true, but would they be any
worse than the blunders of politicians whose own political
existence depends so much on keeping the poor in their
place? Experts are needed to administer the poverty
programs—fine, but in many jurisdictions the experts
have already been excluded by the politicians, as was Dr.
Kenneth Clark from HARYOU-ACT in New York. Besides, who has more actual expertise about poverty than
its victims? If the poor were represented they would
squander money—perhaps, but if antipoverty appropriations are merely converted to patronage by the alchemists
who sit in the City Halls, it is hardly a prudential or even
lawful use of these funds.

Though one hopes for change, the critical battle has
been over who controls the money and how these spoils
are to be divided and distributed to bolster the various
elements of the political establishment. In Appalachia the
problem is to continue the awarding of contracts for high-
way and other public-works construction in the traditional
way, as patronage. In the Deep South the issue is focused

on whether segregationists will be in charge, although the impact of voter registration of Negroes holds some promise of altering that pattern. In Chicago—which is perhaps the most aggravated example in the nation—poverty appropriations are funneled through the old-time ward apparatus of Mayor Daley's machine. Indeed, Daley's office itself has reported that as of June 1966, more than 8,000 new positions in administration of the war on poverty—not jobs for the poor but new patronage appointments—will have been created. And when, in 1965, Washington refused to transmit antipoverty funds to Chicago because of that city's failure to make even minimal efforts to involve the poor, the President himself is reported to have intervened to release the funds, even though Mayor Daley's compliance was not assured.

In New York City, the war on poverty was at the outset wrested from the hands of competent administrators, and representation of the poor was diverted and delivered to aggrandizers, like the then City Council President Paul Screvane and Congressman Adam Powell. *Both* of them are protégés of the old-line white political establishment: Screvane, because he diligently and loyally worked his way up from the precinct and his first patronage job as a Sanitation Department worker; and Powell, because while capitalizing on his own charisma to build a personal following in Harlem, mastered the political skills exemplified by a white Tammany Hall and has employed these skills alternately to collaborate with white politicians or to emasculate them. Screvane and Powell thus had the audacity to squabble in public about how to split the spoils between the "downtown" and the "uptown" politicians, but whether the poor themselves would be represented was never a serious issue between them.

Indeed, Screvane, in his anxiety about the organization of community action groups on the Lower East Side, under the aegis of Mobilization For Youth, resorted to the smear accusation of Communist infiltration in order to abort the effort of MFY to actually enlist the poor in antipoverty efforts at a neighborhood level. It was a tactic which, unhappily, succeeded, to Screvane's discredit, and MFY seems thereby to have been destroyed as an effective antipoverty program.

Meanwhile, another form of patronage has emerged in the vastly expanded openings created for the professional social work bureaucracy, sometimes interlaced with the more conventional political patronage. In its first operational year, for instance, the domestic Peace Corps succeeded in assembling an administrative staff larger than the number of volunteers recruited to work in the field.

These are some of the reasons why it is doubtful that Americans have, as yet, the moral capability to do away with poverty.

The Law and the Poor

If the politicians can and should be criticized as parasites of the poor, so can the other professions—medicine, education, journalism, civil service, the clergy, unionized labor, business of all sorts, investment banking, social work, the law, and, for that matter, organized crime. Perhaps some—like social work or education or the law—have relatively more concern for the poor than others, but the greater contributions are made by poets—and the saints—who live among the poor. In any case, the indifference or animosity of one profession toward the poor provides no excuse for the defaults or failures of the others.

The moral decadence which prevents this society from overcoming poverty is illustrated with special relevance in the realm of law. I speak with extra emphasis because it is my own profession. The law—in its making, enforcement, administration, practice, and adjudication—has virtually abandoned the poor. It fails to counsel them in their complaints; it refuses to represent them in their causes of action; it neglects their rights as citizens, consigning them to charlatans or charity; it is almost totally indifferent to their entrapment in poverty.

Every time one of the Northern urban ghettos explodes, however, there are pious outcries from political bosses, editorial writers, and clergy, who should know better, all wringing their hands and calling for a respect for law. But what law have the ghetto poor known that is worthy of respect? It is time to recognize that there is now an almost complete collapse of confidence in the law on the part of the poor; more and more, the ghetto people are tempted to take the law into their own hands.

What accounts for this? Occasionally there is some traumatic and notorious incident which dramatizes the estrangement between the law and the poor—a Negro teenager is killed by an off-duty white cop, a boy who is poor is forced to confess to abominable crimes he did not commit—but such cases by themselves do not account for the deep and basic hostility that exists. It is, rather, that each such case summons to the memories of the poor all those common, redundant, and apparently trivial complaints which make up their experience of what the law means in practice: rent gouging, vermin infestation, usury, installment credit rackets, lack of water or heat, the

endurance of verbal or minor physical abuse at the hands
of the police, the obstacles to obtaining bail if you are
Negro, various impediments to registration and voting,
being forced to plead guilty because it is more convenient
for the court if you do—and if you don't and are found
guilty, it will be all the worse—the unavailability of
remedies in domestic relations because it simply costs too
much to get a legal separation or divorce. Every such case
only serves to recall all the numberless, anonymous, and
supposedly minor matters, through the generations, in
which those who are poor and those who are black in
American society have suffered indignity, persecution,
discrimination, and harassment in one way or another
under the auspices of the law. For the ghetto poor, in
brief, the law is a symbol of their rejection by society.

Is there a breakdown of law and order in the inner city?
Is there crime in the subways and violence in the streets?
Are the police sometimes assaulted when they try to make
arrests? Are there riots in Watts and Cleveland and
Rochester and skirmishes in Springfield and Roxbury and
Woodlawn? Will next season be long and hot, volatile
and bloody? Answer all such questions in the affirmative
—but then ask—*why*?

The answer is that the accumulation of grievances
against the law—and how it has been made and administered for so long—has become more than can any
longer be endured. Besides, what is to be lost? The worst
that can happen is that one would be killed, and if one is a
ghetto person in America one is already as good as dead.

If any are dissatisfied with such answers, if any wish to
affirm the meaningfulness of law, first destroy the Northern
ghettos and those forces that would perpetuate them.
For the internal state of the ghetto is fundamentally one

of chaos, which imminently threatens to descend into anarchy.

What is frightening in the present situation is that just as a fatal unrest is overtaking the citizens of the ghetto, the recalcitrance of the rest of society is hardening, and the public authorities are beset by what can only be described as hysteria. Apparently the public authorities have been so accustomed to inertia in relation to the ghetto that when today the problems of the ghetto can no longer be rationalized or hidden, their instinct is to stomp out the trouble by naked violence.

Such was the case in the Harlem riots of 1964. The authorization was given, when the early incidents occurred, for the police to fire their weapons to disperse the people congregating on the streets. The initial decision was the most extreme that could have been made. Not fire hoses, not mounted police, not tear gas, but first of all guns—that was the way chosen to subdue the rioters. You may be confident that this came as no surprise to anybody in Harlem. There, as in the other black ghettos of the North, the police have long since functioned as an occupation army. It is not just that a place like Harlem is very heavily policed, although it is—every corner is guarded; every movement is under surveillance; a stranger entering the ghetto is strenuously advised to turn back; even long-time residents of the neighborhood are often detained and interrogated about their business. This is the sort of thing that has been going on for a long time now, which makes Harlem an occupied territory.

Obviously, all policemen are not racists or brutes; many probably do not approve of what they do. No doubt there are policemen who are sadists, but they are not typical. I have also known police officers who were extraordinarily knowledgeable and compassionate, but they are not typical, either. Most policemen are working men who, in order to keep their jobs and, perhaps, win promotions, obey orders. More crucial is the mentality which informs the assignment and conduct of the police in the ghettos and which regards the racial crisis as essentially a military problem, not an issue of civil rights for all citizens. The chief operational objective of police headquarters seems to be to confine the residents of the ghetto and to keep them quiet, to prevent them from leaving the area unless they are going to work, to disperse them if many of them gather in one spot within the ghetto, to keep everyone moving, to make the police presence felt by conspicuous deployment of patrols and paddy wagons and the ostentatious display and handling of weapons, and to err on the side of making false arrests if things seem tense. If, after all such "preventive" measures fail (as I believe they sooner or later must) and riot erupts, there is a determination at all costs to suppress the violence most efficiently by localizing it inside the ghetto so as not to disrupt the rest of society.

The answer to riot is not more cops. The racial crisis, specifically in the black ghettos, will never be resolved by ever more eager and anxious resort to force and by ever greater escalation of police power. Did Watts, with its huge fatalities—or the other sixteen ghetto riots in 1964 and 1965—teach the nation nothing? Shall the militia be summoned for permanent duty in the ghettos to maintain what, euphemistically, would be called "peace" and "order"?

This is what is coming if this society is not diverted from the present collision course in which it has been set by the response of the established authorities in the principal cities to the violence which has already occurred. That is what is morally certain unless the legitimate discontent of the ghetto people is answered with fundamental redress rather than reliance upon the superiority in firepower of the police against rioters.

The police and the lower courts do not deserve all blame for the hostility between the poor and the law. Practicing lawyers and the law schools share much of the responsibility. For a very, very long time, the poor have not been represented in their legal causes because their cases are unremunerative and have been regarded by lawyers as vulgar, offensive, or unimportant. Urban lawyers, perhaps especially in the larger firms, tend to abhor the kind of cases which have the highest incidence in slum neighborhoods—narcotics addiction, domestic nonsupport, harassment by landlords, juvenile crime, housing violations—and have thereby left those who have such problems either unrepresented or with no other recourse but to shysters, political clubhouse lawyers, or charity.

In many jurisdictions there is charity, usually the Legal Aid Society. My experience indicates that Legal Aid does a creditable job in representing the indigent, but the fantastic caseload of Legal Aid comes nowhere near coping with the vast numbers of poor people who go unrepresented—and have been for generations—because they cannot afford a lawyer. Meanwhile, it is condescension, rather than a sufficient discharge of the public responsibility of the legal profession, for a law firm to donate a few dollars to the Legal Aid Society as its way of representing those who are poor.

Even more disturbing—and conclusive—as evidence of the moral apathy of the law toward the poor is that the chief opposition, in several major urban jurisdictions, to the institution of public defender offices which would provide counsel in criminal proceedings and be the equivalent on the defense side of the public prosecutor's office, has come from within the legal profession. More than that, despite some provisions through the war on poverty and also through private foundations for experimental "neighborhood" law clinics in some ghetto areas, such recent efforts to provide more adequate representation for the poor have met with massive opposition from practicing lawyers and from some bar associations.

New Haven, Connecticut, a city which is famed for its supposed pioneering ventures in urban renewal and anti-poverty efforts, was the scene of an extremely acrimonious fight within the local bar association against providing counsel through a neighborhood program to the poor, although neither those law firms supporting the venture nor those opposed to it had been actually and conscientiously involved in representing the New Haven poor at all, except for some occasional gesture of charity. In one Ohio city, it was only after a major race riot that some of the leaders of the bar association and of the local law schools decided that the representation of the poor before the law was significant in the war against poverty, and undertook a program to provide it.

Already, mutterings are heard in the profession about "socialized law," despite the venerable dictum in American jurisprudence that even the least in society are entitled to counsel and to equality before the law.

At the same time, legal education for more than three decades has pursued a specialization that has equipped the legal profession to serve the great corporate powers, the government, and the prosperous, but has relegated the preparation of lawyers in matters of civil rights, juvenile crime, domestic relations, tenant problems and the like to the periphery of the curriculum. It has seemed important to the law schools to train members of the profession to serve property rights, even to the neglect of human rights. It has been thought more urgent to require that all law students know accounting than that they be trained to insure that the ethical assumptions of American society are upheld and that the poor are assured legal representation and the equal protection of the law.

The default of the legal profession and of legal education with respect to the poor jeopardizes the whole of society, not just the poor. If the least in society—whoever they may be at a particular time or in specific circumstances: the Negro, the politically unpopular, the social deviate, the American Indian, the immigrant, the poor, the migrant farmer—are unable, as a practical matter, to secure representation in their complaints, rights, causes, and self-interests in society, the American idea of society is compromised for everybody. It would mean that one is entitled to legal representation only by virtue of class or wealth or race or sex or other status. If equality before the law is not functional—that is, readily accessible and viable as a remedy for a citizen's grievance or assertion of his rights—it is a fantasy even for those who have it and use it as a matter of privilege or purchase.

In no other realm are the ethics of American society more solemnly challenged than in this. Nowhere has the law more compromised American society; in no other sector is the rule of law more immediately threatened; in no other work can the law find vindication, if, indeed, there is still time for that.

Sin, Morality, and Poverty

The moral complacency of most citizens in regard to poverty is largely due to the success this society has achieved in keeping the poor out of sight: the mind is not appalled by conditions the eyes have not seen; the conscience is not moved by what the nostrils have not inhaled.

Concealment, indeed, is one synonym for ghettoization. Whether the concealment of poverty in urban society has been wickedly calculated I doubt, although the consistency and similarity of the patterns of concealment throughout the country make that a fascinating hypothesis. More likely, as far as most middle-class citizens are concerned, the poor have been put out of sight almost inadvertently; very often this has been done in the name of renewal and for the sake of civic improvement. Thus the reconstruction of the central city in Minneapolis caused the relocation of the old downtown Negro ghetto to another part of the city. It seems as if in one stroke the blight of the downtown area has been removed and the Negroes have vanished. In Buffalo, the new thruway to handle the increased traffic from the white suburbs to the business district has been constructed right over the roofs of the tenements, quite effectively and very effectually hiding the ghetto and literally burying its residents. In principle, the same approach has been taken in almost every city.

The concealment of poverty by ghettoization of the poor means that both prosperous and poor live so separately and have so little human contact of any kind, are so accustomed to acting out a charade instead, that each regards the other in stereotypes which seldom contain much truth. The most popular stereotype of the poor is that in America a person is poor by choice and not because of circumstances beyond his own influence. Thus, if the poor were not so lazy, they would not be poor. If the poor were not so promiscuous, they would be able to support themselves. If the poor were not so profligate in drugs and drink and other dissipations, they would escape from their misery. These are the common variations of the same theme that accounts for poverty as proof of moral decadence. Driven to its ultimate logic, to be poor is a grave sin. Such a stereotype of the poor is credible and popular among the prosperous because it implies that to be prosperous is a sign of moral superiority.

Neither side of the stereotype is true, however, either empirically or theologically. Poverty, like wealth—in America as elsewhere—is more often a matter of inheritance and coincidence than of choice or initiative.

Apart from a few of those saints, I have yet to meet a man who elected to be poor, and I have never met an affluent man whose estate could be truthfully accounted for as his own individual accomplishment. If one is born an American Indian—for instance in Oklahoma, where most Indians subsist on governmental charity—the chances are about three to one that one will, like his forefathers, remain confined to a reservation, never have his intelligence or other capabilities recognized or utilized, be deprived of any education qualifying him to leave the reservation and secure and hold outside employment, or, in turn, be able to locate a habitable place to live off the reservation, enter a church, obtain a loan, be bonded, open a charge account, secure a license from public agencies, or even conveniently get a haircut. Much the same is the lot of the offspring of migrant crop workers in California, in New England, in Virginia, in upstate New York, and elsewhere in the country, or, to take another example, of the heirs of miners who have been unemployable for a generation in Appalachia. And, if one is an American Negro male and is born in the ghetto, it is probable that one will die in the ghetto.

This stereotype that the poor are morally deficient and that, therefore, their poverty is their own fault, is particularly asserted at the present time as a desperate rationalization for the denial of equal rights in society to Negro citizens in the Northern cities. The argument is that many ethnic groups have immigrated to this country —Jews and Poles and Hungarians and Italians and Portuguese and Irish and Germans—and while suffering some discrimination and conflicts, have gradually and successfully been absorbed and accepted in American society. Parts of Harlem used to be immigrant slums—those other groups escaped from the slums and have "made it" in this country; why haven't the Negroes done the same? The answer, unhappily, is ludicrously obvious; it is also very sad and terrible. The answer is that the pattern of assimilation in urban life of immigrants from other nations has not been applicable to Negro citizens because Negroes are *not* immigrants. Apart from the Indians, they are the earliest Americans, arriving as they did, however reluctantly, three centuries ago when the slave trade to the North American continent began. They have a venerable and utterly unique American ancestry that no others—of all the varieties of language, nationality, or race which have come to America—can claim or approximate. Moreover, the precedent of immigrant assimilation in the great Northern cities has not applied to Negro citizens because *white supremacy has been the dominant ethic in virtually every realm of society in America for the past three hundred years and remains entrenched even today.* In 1966, of course, it is often a *de facto,* patronizing racism, more subtle than in the days of chattel slavery or of militant segregation in the post-Civil War era, but it has remained effective enough to imprison and immobilize multitudes of Negroes for generations in the urban North. Immigrants from Europe surely had trials and travails on coming to these shores, but they never threatened by their presence or challenged by their conduct the ethic of white supremacy. Thus their eventual assimilation was not hindered, once language barriers had been muted, cultural distinctions diluted, and religious and nationalistic prejudices challenged. It is white supremacy—not moral inferiority, and not choice—that accounts for the black ghettos.

One of the ironies for those among the white and the prosperous who fondly preach free enterprise and individual initiative as the virtues which, no doubt they can be, is that racial supremacy is so manifestly inconsistent with these ideas. It is an extravagant hypocrisy for white people who are well off to scold Negroes who are not, for lack of enterprise after having kept them for so long in servitude, then in separation, and now locked up in the slums. Whites cannot really have it both ways: If they cherish freedom of initiative, they must forgo white supremacy; if they have more affection for the latter, let them at least forbear from denouncing those whom they oppress.

One corollary of the racial and class separation of society is the notion that whatever the legitimate needs of the poor, they can be met through private philanthropy. However, this assumes that—despite their radical separation from the poor—the prosperous are enlightened and compassionate enough to make need the measure of their charity. But the concealment of poverty from those who are not poor refutes such an assumption. Such reasoning also takes for granted that organized charity is seriously committed to the service of human need, a premise which is difficult to defend if one considers the diversion of charitable contributions to the financing of expensive promotions and self-serving bureaucracies. Institutionalized private charity is a monster, exploiting human suffering in appeals to the crudest motivations, with much of the money going to the professional fund-raisers rather than to heal the sick, comfort the afflicted, or accomplish much of any practical charity at all. The truth is that private institutionalized charity in America has now become so heavily oriented toward its own maintenance that it has little left over to meet the empirical needs of those whom it purports to help. All the while, a spirit of condescension is cultivated that corrupts the good intentions of the prosperous and nurtures a spirit of despair that demeans recipients of charity as human beings. To put it bluntly, private charity has simply become too fat, too introverted, too manipulative of both donors and named beneficiaries to commend it as a sensible way of resolving any of the substantive issues of American poverty.

Theologically, the dual stereotype of the poor as morally defective and the prosperous as morally excellent is objectionable as a crude doctrine of justification by works, which ignores the fact that there is an obvious interdependence between rich and poor. To use an ordinary example, most white people in this society are investors in life and property insurance. On the surface, this seems a prudent and morally innocent action in which a man takes some precautions against certain predictable risks for the benefit of his family or himself. At the same time, I suppose, most white folks—at least theoretically—disapprove of slums and would just as soon see them vanish from the cities. Yet the lives of men are so entangled in this world that there *is* a relationship between the purchase of insurance, on one hand, and the preservation of slums, on the other.

Insurance companies in many jurisdictions are restricted as to their permissible investments; real estate is one of those commonly allowed. In the great cities insurance companies have become substantial speculators in real estate, and the impact of their manipulations has contributed to the demolition of some blighted sections, the dispossession of tenants from the site, and the reconstruction of the site into commercial or residential properties that the dispossessed legally cannot afford or are not entitled to occupy. Thus the slum dweller is driven deeper into the ghetto, and the slums become fewer but worse. I am not advocating that all conscientious citizens divest themselves of insurance policies because their insurers may be involved in real estate speculations that aggravate the slums, but the beginning of conscience, in a Christian sense, is realizing that every action or omission, even those which seem routine and trivial, is consequentially related to the lives of all other human beings on the face of the earth. Even the typical prudent act of buying insurance is not morally innocuous but extremely ambiguous, and entangles one man in the existence of others in many ways unintended and, as yet, unknown. The same sort of thing can be said, in principle, of any form of investment or saving, not just insurance, which is something trustees of church and college endowments might keep more promi-

nently in mind if they are not to continue to practice the
blatant hypocrisy of investing in enterprises that contra-
dict what the churches preach and the colleges teach. Conscience, in other words, is knowing that men are related to,
and responsible for, each other in all things. That is why
poverty cannot be accounted for by blaming it on the poor,
since the prosperous are proximately involved in the institutionalization of poverty in society.

Poverty and Ideology

The moral stamina to utilize the resources and technology of this society to abolish poverty begins in the
awakening of conscience and in the commitment of citizens to some fundamental idea of society.

No reference is made here to those ideological conflicts
which preoccupy so much public attention but which have
so little substantive significance for the nation. In other
words, the conflict as to the form of society in America
is not, as nearly as I can make out, capitalism *vs* communism. Few citizens, I suspect, could be intelligently
articulate about the differences between them, in terms of
economic theory, and the matter becomes truly theoretical
because neither system exists in practice in the developed
countries of the modern world.

Contemporary Soviet society bears about as little re-
semblance to classical Marxism as modern American
society does to laissez-faire capitalism. Those in the Soviet
Union and the United States who mourn such mutations
of, and departures from, ideological doctrine are at least
responding appropriately: both communism and capitalism *are* dead. Meanwhile, China, which, significantly, is

increasingly considered both as the hobgoblin of American vested interests in Southeast Asia and the competitor of Soviet vested interests throughout the Eastern world, is more plausibly comprehended in terms of the traditional hegemony of an emerging great power.

Classically, of course, both capitalism and communism emerge as responses to the Industrial Revolution, which began in Europe two centuries ago and which quickly matured in the United States. Whatever the merits of either in their origination, both were addressed to conditions of primitive industrialization that no longer prevail in this nation or, one gathers, in Europe, the Soviet Union, and Japan. The realities which America in the middle of the twentieth century confronts are those of a mass, urbanized, automated, cybernated society. In regard to those realities, however they may be dealt with, both capitalism and communism are ideologically obsolete, and it is morally and intellectually dissipating to engage the attention and energies of society in an endless sham battle over ideas which have been superseded by advances in science and technology that were not even imagined at the inception of either capitalism or communism. For the present realities, both of these ideologies seem too old-fashioned and reactionary.

If the ideological conflict between capitalism and communism is ridiculous in the United States today, inasmuch as neither practically exists nor could be established, and if that struggle saps the moral strength of the nation by distracting citizens from urgent actual problems, that does not mean there are no serious ideological differences among us. On the contrary, the country still suffers from the same ideological split which divided the nation in the first place. The authentically American ideological controversy, still unresolved, is concerned over which is more suitable as the constitution of society—the rights of property or the rights of human beings.

That dispute, of course, was embodied in some of the pre-Revolutionary protests, and later in the squabbles between Jefferson and Hamilton. It emerged again in the debate over whether property was to be a condition of suffrage and elective office, in the abolitionist movement, somewhat belatedly in the campaign for woman suffrage, and eventually in the labor revolution. It is raised again nowadays, of course, in the civil rights movement and the war on poverty, but also in other realms, for example in the impact of technological change upon work, and in the universities, where money remains the principal qualification for entrance into higher education.

I had supposed—naïvely, as it turns out—that the American ideological struggle had been settled irrevocably a century ago by the Civil War. Even taking into consideration all the other skirmishes before and since, it was that momentous division of the nation that dramatized the issue of property *vs* persons most terribly and most bluntly. After all, *ideologically,* what was the Civil War about? It was about whether certain human beings are property or persons: if chattels, then society belongs to those who acquire, possess, or control property; if persons, then human rights, verified by nothing more than being a human being, have precedence in society over property.

Subsequent events demonstrate that the American ideological conflict was not decisively settled by the Civil War; at the very least, the struggle continues. The crises of poverty, race, and technology in contemporary America have provoked a strenuous resurgence in the advocacy of mere property rights as the basis of society. Some argue, of course, that the acquisition and possession of property itself represents a human right from which all other rights are appropriately derived. It is a self-serving argument—persuasive only to those already privileged with money and other forms of property, or to those who labor under the illusion that someday they will somehow accumulate property.

Whether this American ideological conflict will ever be resolved and, if so, whether property or persons will be subordinated, one to the other, remains in doubt. Whatever the outcome, I contend that insofar as the property ethic prevails, our idea of democracy will have been forfeited and the nation deprived of the moral authority to banish poverty.

Property, Money, and the Ethics of Society

The popular fascination with property as the fundamental institution of society is fixed in America upon the symbol of money.

A Christian who is also an American can hardly be unaware of the special irony involved in his attempt to analyze the meaning of money, both socially and theologically. A banker or money-changer might wish to disqualify me from having any views—just because I do not happen to have any money to boast of. But is it not the truth that those who do not have money know as much about its meaning as those who possess it? On the other hand, a pauper or beggar might complain that it is gratuitous to speak of money if one is, as I am, a young, white, Anglo-Saxon, Episcopalian, Harvard attorney, for whom obtaining a position, accumulating money, and acquiring

whatever money can buy takes no remarkable effort. The
subject is compelling for me precisely because in this
society it is simple for some to make money if they choose
to do so, while very difficult for others.

One is haunted by the impression that, for Christians, if
not for other men, the issues of money and property of all
sorts were long ago settled. Heed these examples:

Jesus admonished the rich young man who sought justification to dispose of what he had and give it to the poor
and thereby follow Christ. Is that warning now forgotten?

Jesus purified the temple when it had become a haven
for thieves. Is that no precedent for the Church?

Jesus was nursed in a shed, did not follow the occupation of his father Joseph but became an itinerant, had no
place to sleep, sought out the poor and disadvantaged, and
blessed them many times and in many ways. He was seldom welcomed among the affluent; by all accounts He was
poor Himself in every worldly sense, and declared that
money belongs to Caesar. Where the Church and the
people of the Church forsake His poverty, is not Christ
thereby foresworn?

Although money and the property which money begets
accomplishes, in America, fabulous and terrifying feats, no
camel has yet passed through the eye of a needle.

After all, the price, in money, of the life of Christ was
thirty coins.

No attack is intended on so-called "materialism," in the
sense in which that term is so often juxtaposed to so-called
"spiritual values." In the Gospel of Christ there is no
dichotomy between "material" and "spiritual." Indeed,
the realities to which these words refer in the Gospel do

not exist separately, in distinction one from the other, or in opposition to one another—although that was what the Greeks supposed and what many Americans still vainly assume. In the Gospel, these are made one, each indispensable to the other, each inherent in the other. The very event of the Incarnation concerns the reconciliation in the world of the realities which men call "material" and "spiritual." Since the Incarnation, for men to persist in thinking and speaking of "material" *vs* "spiritual" is not only a sign of confusion but is also both false and profane.

Neither is it in any way here implied that money or other forms of property are intrinsically evil. Though certain religions have that view and though some preachers in Christendom share it, the Gospel does not support it. In the Christian faith, rather, money is known as one of the institutions of this world which, like all other principalities and powers, is fallen. This means simply that money has lost its essential integrity as an institution, and exists in a state of distortion as to its true meaning and function; it is now both symbol and fact of the alienation which exists between and among all men and all principalities in this world. Money is not inherently evil, but it *is* fallen: in other words, it is subject to death, along with everything and everyone else in creation.

By the same token, the owning of money is, in and of itself, no sin (if that provides any comfort to those who may have some of it). Where sin enters in, instead, is how men and institutions regard money and, hence, both in and how people and institutions use money and in how money uses them.

Perhaps the moral ambiguity of money is most plainly evidenced in the popular belief that money itself has value and that the worth of other things or of men is somehow measured in monetary terms, rather than the other way around, where money is considered only to have value rendered to it by things or men. Whatever the case in earlier times or in other cultures, the view that money has a worth of its own, from which other things or from which persons derive their worth, is by now deeply embedded in the folk mentality of Americans.

The other night, to take a bizarre example, I watched a film on television concerning an exploration in a remote and primitive land undertaken by some Americans in search of gold. The movie portrayed the indigenous people of the island as a superstitious and ignorant lot, sitting on top of the fabulous treasure which they did nothing to exploit, believing that it belonged to some unknown and fearful god. The Americans required the services of a native guide to lead them to the hoard, but all of their initial attempts to persuade one of the island residents to do so could not overcome the local superstition. Then one bright American, as a last resort it seemed, offered to pay a native two hundred dollars in American money—he made a great point of it being *American* money—if the native would be the guide. Behold, what had been represented as generations of inbred fear and legend departed from the native and he eagerly made the bargain, though on his island there was not a transistor radio, much less an air conditioner, that he could purchase with this bribe. The proposition in the film was, of course, that the money itself was valuable.

Any number of other instances that represent the same regard for money as something of original worth come to mind. One Christmas, I recall, I gave a book to a boy of fifteen. He is the son of a family well known to me, with whom gifts are always exchanged on such occasions as

Christmas. The family is not wealthy, but it is privileged, having all of the possessions—cars and boats and appliances, often in duplicate—which are assumed essentials to middle-class status in America. Both parents are college graduates, they have a modest library in their household, it is not uncommon for each of them to read and to be observed doing so by their children. The boy himself attends an academically excellent public school and, while no genius, is a bright and energetic person. He knows that I myself write books and I once overheard him brag to a friend of his that he knew me, a real, live author, much as he might boast of knowing a professional baseball player. Anyway, I gave the boy a book for Christmas. Later on, he asked me why I had given him a book—why hadn't I given him something worthwhile—why hadn't I given him money instead? There ensued a long, candid and, to me, fascinating discussion about books and money. The boy's view was that books are written by people to make money; books are read, if required, in school or in a job in order, sooner or later, to make money; if someday one had enough money one might purchase many books, along with other furnishings, and one might even, then, read books for diversion (presumably to have something to do to break the monotony of counting money). The only book which this boy would welcome as a gift is a bankbook. I do not blame the boy himself, or his parents, or his teachers. I am pretty sure there is much more involved in his attitude toward money than can be so simply attributed. And, of course, it occurs to me that he has seen *that* stupid movie, too, or a hundred others like it, and that in this and a host of other ways he has heard the word that it is money which is in itself the only valuable thing.

One does not have to mingle with the privileged, however, to learn how fondly money is heeded in American society. One may as well ask the poor about it. The idea that money has integral value is popular among the poor and is—ironically—the incentive for much of their own exploitation. There have been those, for example, who have for generations profiteered off the Harlem Negroes by a macabre traffic in phony cosmetics, particularly so-called skin bleaches and hair straighteners. Part of the appeal and economic success of such enterprises has been the very cost of the item. The notion propagated is that an expensive product must surely be what it is represented to be. And while the exploitation of racism in the advertising and merchandising of such cosmetics has now significantly subsided, in the ghetto economy the practice still survives of overpricing goods in order to sell them, relying upon the common belief of customers that price in money indicates value. I know Harlem merchants who admit that the easiest way to push certain slow-selling items is to up the price tag without regard for the wholesale cost, since many people, perhaps especially the poor, are easily persuaded to buy, being already predisposed to the belief that the purchase price represents real value.

Whether among the prosperous or among the poor, the same basic notion usually prevails: *money equals value.* What something or someone costs is what something or someone is worth intrinsically. Money can secure status, preference, notoriety, power. Money can open most any door. Money is all-important because, in fact, almost everyone *does* have a price. Money is due honor because money is the arbiter of value, not only in tangible ways, where matters of goods or properties are involved, but also in the more intangible realms, where prestige and position are at stake. In either case, it is money which is the idol.

The Idolatry of Money

Inordinate covetousness is not the main issue, however; in many cultures men have given over their lives to the accumulation of wealth. The more somber issue, both socially and theologically, is the idolatry of money.

Idolatry, whatever its object, represents the enshrinement of any other person or thing in the place of God Himself. Idolatry embraces some person or thing, instead of God, as the source and rationalization of the moral significance of this life in the world for, at least, the idolater, though not, necessarily, for anybody else at all. Thus men, as idolaters, have from time to time worshiped stones and snakes and suns and fire and thunder, their own dreams and hallucinations, images of themselves and of their progenitors; they have had all the Caesars, ancient and modern, as idols; others have fancied sex as a god; for many, race is an idol; some worship science, some idolize superstition. Within that pantheon, money is a most conspicuous idol.

The idolatry of money means that the moral worth of a man is judged in terms of the amount of money he possesses or controls. The acquisition and accumulation of money in itself is considered evidence of virtue. It does not so much matter how money is acquired—by work or invention, through inheritance or marriage, by luck or theft—the main thing is to get some. The corollary of this doctrine, of course, is that those without money are morally inferior—weak, or indolent, or otherwise less worthy as men. Where money is an idol, to be poor is a sin.

This is an obscene idea of justification, directly in contradiction with the Bible. In the Gospel no man is saved by any works of his own, least of all by the mere acquisition of money. In fact, the New Testament is redundant in citing the possession of riches as an impediment to salvation when money is regarded idolatrously. At the same time, the notion of justification by acquisition of money is empirically absurd, for it oversimplifies the relationship of the prosperous and the poor and overlooks the dependence of the rich upon the poor for their wealth. In this world men live at each other's expense, and the affluence of the few is proximately related to, and supported by, the poverty of the many.

This interdependence of rich and poor is something Americans are tempted to overlook, since so many Americans are in fact prosperous, but it is true today as it was in earlier times: the vast multitudes of men on the face of the earth are consigned to poverty for their whole lives, without any serious prospect whatever of changing their conditions. Their hardships in great measure make possible the comfort of those who are not poor; their poverty maintains the luxury of others; their deprivation purchases the abundance most Americans take for granted.

That leaves prosperous Americans with frightful questions to ask and confront, even in customs or circumstances which are regarded as trivial or straightforward or settled. Where, for instance, do the profits that enable great corporations to make large contributions to universities and churches and charity come from? Do they come from the servitude of Latin American peasants working plantations on 72-hour weekly shifts for gross annual incomes of less than a hundred dollars? Do they depend upon the availability of black child labor in South Africa and Rhodesia? Are such private beneficences in fact the real earnings of some of the poor of the world?

To affirm that men live in this world at each other's expense is a confession of the truth of the Fall rather than an assertion of economic doctrine or a precise empirical statement. It is not that there is in every transaction a direct one-for-one cause and effect relationship, either individually or institutionally, between the lot of the poor and the circumstances of those who are not poor. It is not that the wealthy are wicked or that the fact of malice is implicit in affluence. It is, rather, theologically speaking, that all human and institutional relationships are profoundly distorted and so entangled that no man or principality in this world is innocent of involvement in the existence of all men and all institutions. It is the affirmation in a society like the United States, which is possessed of enough wealth of all kinds to insure everyone a decent existence, that moral responsibility is initiated in the realization that this is a fallen world in which the alienation of institutions and men means an extraordinary intensification of their interdependence.

Those who would try to account for American prosperity by simplistic rationalizations about ingenuity, initiative, or the favor of God, or those who credit their own wealth merely to their own diligence, enterprising spirit, or even luck, should try to live with their families on a Welfare subsistence check. Indeed, every American would be wise to remember how dependent their earnings are on cheap, plentiful labor. Huge profits are guaranteed by the prevalence of poverty in a particular area, indeed by the deliberate maintenance of multitudes of human beings in ignorance and servitude in Africa, Asia, Latin America—and, for that matter, in Natchez, Mississippi, Albuquerque, New Mexico, and Washington, D.C. Each time a prosperous American peels a banana, let him remember the peon who picked it; whenever a housewife uses a pan, let her recall that the copper from which it was made was probably mined by slaves; the next time a middle-class citizen pays an insurance premium, let him intercede for the people of the ghettos.

The idolatry of money has its most grotesque form as a doctrine of immortality. Money is, then, not only evidence of the present moral worth of a person, but also the way in which his life gains moral worth after death. If a man leaves a substantial estate, death is cheated of victory for a while, if not ultimately defeated, because the money he leaves will sustain the memory of the man and of his fortune. The poor just die and are at once forgotten. It is supposed important to amass money not for its use in life but as a monument in death. Money thus becomes the measure of a man's moral excellence while he lives and the means to purchase a certain survival of death. Money makes men not only moral but immortal; that is the most profound and popular idolatry of money.

To the Christian conscience, all ideas of immortality— along with all notions of self-justification including that of the mere acquisition of money or other property—are anathema. The Gospel of Jesus Christ is not concerned with immortality but with the resurrection from death; not with the survival of death either in some "afterlife" or in the memorialization of life after death. The Gospel is, instead, distinguished by the transcendence of the power of death here and now within the precincts of life in this world. The Gospel discerns and exposes *all* forms of idolatry as the worship of death, and, thus, the Gospel recognizes and publicizes the idolatry of money or property in any form as both false and futile. False because

where money is an idol—that is, where money is thought
to impute great or even ultimate moral significance to the
one who holds it—it pre-empts the place of God; futile
because money, and everything whatsoever that money
can buy or build or do, along with men who lust after or
gain money, dies. Where money is beheld as an idol, in
truth the idol which is secreted in such worship is death.
The Gospel is about resurrection and it is that which un-
masks the fraudulent association of all promissory doc-
trines of immortality with idolatry in one or another
fashion. The Gospel, in other words, has to do with the
readily available power of God's grace to emancipate men
in this life from all idols of death, even money—and even
in America.

It is the freedom from idolatry of money that Christ
offers the rich young man in the parable. Remember, it is
not that money is inherently evil, or that the possession
of money as such is sin. The issue for the Christian (and
ultimately, for everyone) is whether a man trusts money
more than God, and comes to rely on money rather than
on grace for the assurance of his moral significance, both
as an individual and in his relations with the whole of
mankind.

As a Christian I am aware—with more intimate knowledge and, therefore, with even greater anguish than those
outside the Church—that the churches in American
society nowadays are so much in the position of that rich
young man in the parable that they are rarely in a position
to preach to prosperous Americans, much less to the
needy. Even where the churches are not engaged in
deliberate idolatry of money, the overwhelming share of
the resources in money and other property inherited by
and given to the trust of the churches ends up being utilized

just for the upkeep of the ecclesiastical establishment.
Appeals are still being made that to give money to the
churches is equivalent to giving money to God. Of course
anyone, if he cares to, or if he is free to do so, can see
through such a claim: it is just a modern—albeit less
candid, yet more vulgar—sale of indulgences, an abuse
against which there is a venerable history of protest beginning with Jesus Himself when He evicted the money-
changers from the temple.

Freedom from idolatry of money, for a Christian, means
that money becomes useful only as a sacrament—as a
sign of the restoration of life wrought in this world by
Christ. The sacramental use of money has little to do with
supporting the Church after the manner of contributing
to conventional charities, and even less with the self-
styled stewardship that solicits funds mainly for the maintenance of ecclesiastical salaries and the housekeeping of
churchly properties. The Church and the Church's mission
do not represent another charity to be subsidized as a
necessary or convenient benevolence, or as a moral
obligation, or in order to reassure the prosperous that they
are either generous or righteous. Appeals for Church support as charity or for maintenance commonly end up
abetting the idolatry of money.

Such idolatry is regularly dramatized in the offertory,
where it is regarded as "the collection" and as an inter-
mission in the worship of the people of the congregation.
Actually, the offertory is integral to the sacramental existence of the Church, a way of representing the oblation
of the totality of life to God. No more fitting symbol of
the involvement of Christians in the everyday life of the
world could be imagined, in American society at least,
than money, for nearly every relationship in personal and

public life is characterized by the obtaining or spending or exchange of money. If then, in worship, men offer themselves and all of their decisions, actions, and words to God, it is well that they use money as the witness to that offering. Money is, thus, used sacramentally within the Church and not contributed as to some charity or given because the Church, as such, has any need of money.

The sacramental use of money in the formal and gathered worship of the Church is authenticated—as are all other churchly sacramental practices—in the sacramental use of money in the common life of the world.

No end of ways exist in which money can be so appropriated and spent, but, whatever the concrete circumstances, the consistent mark of such a commitment of money is a person's freedom from idolatry of money. That includes not simply freedom from an undue affection for money but, much more than that, freedom from moral dependence upon the pursuit, acquisition, or accumulation of money for the sake of justifying himself or his conduct or actions or opinions, either to himself or to anybody else. It means the freedom to have money, to use money, to spend money without worshiping money, and thus it means the freedom to do without money, if need be, or, having some, to give it away to anyone who seems to need money to maintain life awhile longer.

The charity of Christians, in other words, in the use of money sacramentally—in both the liturgy and in the world—has no serious similarity to conventional charity but is always a specific dramatization of the members of the Body of Christ losing their life in order that the world be given life. For a member of the Church, therefore, it always implies a particular confession that his money is

not his own because his life is not his own, but, by the
example of God's own love, belongs to the world.

That one's own life belongs to the world, that one's
money and possessions, talents and time, influence and
health, all belong to the whole world is, I trust, why the
saints are habitués of poverty and ministers to the outcasts,
friends of the humiliated and, commonly, unpopular themselves. Contrary to many legends, the saints are not spooky
figures, morally superior, abstentious, pietistic. They are
seldom even remembered, much less haloed. In truth, all
men are called to be saints, but that just means called to be
fully human, to be perfect—that is, whole, mature, fulfilled. The saints are simply those men and women who
relish the event of life as a gift and who realize that the
only way to honor such a gift is to give it away.

No doubt some will think all this imprudent and im-
practical, and, in any event, difficult to practice and apt
to be unpopular. But the answer to that is that fidelity to
the Gospel is not measured by the affluence of the Church
but rather by how the Church loves and serves the world
in deploying and spending the wealth the Church happens
at a certain time to have to give. And, for an individual
Christian, the answer to that is that though money be a
beguiling idol and one which is easy to reverence, money
has yet to justify a single human being or secure for him
the freedom to be a person, while there are many men
who, having feared that money or other property is God,
have found it worthless except as evidence against themselves.

Having such a view of money and of its significance
theologically and socially means, of course, that there is
an inherent tension between being a Christian and being
an American citizen. Christians have suffered similar stress

in every secular order in which they have ever been resident. Keep in mind Martin Luther King. Remember Bonhoeffer. Recall Charles Williams. Think of Kierkegaard. Recollect Zwingli. Honor Luther. Take the example of Francis. Be grateful for Augustine. Don't forget Anthony. Behold Paul. Do not overlook James. Recognize Timothy. Celebrate Jesus.

If Christians in America in the present day endure tension because the secular order which we happen to have inherited and in which we happen to live is profoundly alien, peculiarly with respect to its idolatry and temptations to idolatry of property and money, let that be no surprise, for Christians have always suffered that sort of distinction in society.

Theology and Technology

In my mind and in my conscience there is no plan or panacea for the reconstruction of American society in a way in which the precedence of human rights over the rights of property would be secured. I am aware that the civil rights movement, which in so many ways is the conspicuous rallying point of those who advocate human rights in preference to property rights, is, nevertheless, itself ambivalent about property. There are, indeed, some illustrious leaders in the American Negro community who argue that they are not, for now, concerned with the basic moral structure of American society but only with the admission of Negro citizens into the prevailing society. If, as they would put it, Americans are dominated by a decadent middle-class mentality which idolizes property but which is otherwise morally empty, then let the American Negro citizen have his fair share of the emptiness. It is both an appealing and an appalling view: let the corruption of American white society be no excuse to bar Negroes from it; let the poor not wait for help because society is otherwise imperfect; let integration not be postponed while men search for utopia. But I, for one, trust that one stone is still enough to stop two birds, sometimes, and that the vigor and vastness of the Negro revolt and the poignancy and contradiction of the situation of the poor in America will somehow be enough to enable society to be fundamentally reconstructed while the citizenship of Negroes is being vindicated and the grievances of the poor are redressed. I think there is, in fact, such a thing as genuine intercession and that the cause of the Negro citizen and the concomitant need of the whole community of the American poor, both black and white, can somehow be met in a fashion that at the same time redeems the decadence of the great, predominantly white, morally inept, American bourgeoisie.

But how?

Having no panaceas, only some further ventures are commended here:

For one thing, let us forsake the sham battles of ideology and try to address the realities of the *present* American existence—this mass, automated, urbanized, cybernated society, or whatever it should be named.

That surely involves the recognition that the traditional political institutions—the inherited federal system dividing powers largely by happenstance geographical jurisdictions among localities, states, and Washington—are, at least, open to question as a sensible and workable system of self-government. In the New York City complex, for example, an area calculated to embrace all those who are economically interdependent, exist some twenty-five millions of people presently governed by literally hundreds of distinct and uncoordinated agencies, bureaus, authorities, legislatures, executives, and various improvisations of government. That there exists fantastic waste, perpetual corruption, inevitable inefficiency, an excess of patronage, and the resignation of most citizens to bewilderment or apathy is hardly a surprise under the circumstances. What has emerged in such places as New York, I suggest, is a new political reality—a new sort of city-state—as to which the traditional forms of political administration in the federal system are proving themselves inappropriate. New York City is not now governed. Merely replacing a mayor is no remedy if the inherited political institutions, including the mayor's office, are anachronistic. New York City is not governed, principally because the existing political instrumentalities are generically incapable of governing. The federal system is not a *sine qua non* of political democracy and is not sacrosanct to modern urbanization. In fact, the present task is a radical overhaul of the inherited institutions in order to constitute a government for megalopolis that will work, both with some effectiveness and some human concern.

The institutions of public welfare, like those of organized private charity, have substantially failed to reverse, much less resolve, the issues of urban poverty. They represent, in the long run, the most costly means of caring for the poor, both in expense to the taxpayer and in humiliation to the recipient, and, more than that, the bureaucratic overhead, partly because of the patronage interest involved, is out of all proportion to the practical assistance the poor actually receive. Yet few municipal welfare or educational authorities, not to mention private business or labor unions, have yet begun to locate, recruit, educate, and place those who are presently unemployable because of race or lack of acquired skills in occupations apt to survive automation, not because of any technical incapacity to do so, but, apparently, for the absence of any conviction that it must be done.

The answer to an indefinite expansion of public welfare coverage and a continued spiraling of welfare costs is more jobs and the requisite education and training to gainfully employ those who have been deprived of jobs because of inferior education or racial discrimination or technology or any combination of the three. That means, perhaps, a significant reduction of the work week in order to multiply jobs in existing enterprises, together with a vast expansion in the leisure industries, and of employment in those fields due to an increased consumer demand for leisure activities created by a cutback in the work week. The prospects, admittedly, in increasing the number of jobs available in this way is not an altogether happy one. But if, as it now seems, the alternative is the enlargement of the ranks of the unemployable, the continued imprisonment of people in the ghettos and a deepening of their dependence upon public assistance, then so be it.

Technology is both opportunity and threat, but why does the notion persist that whatever technology can do must be done? Just because technological developments can displace a thousand men with a machine does not require that the machine be, in fact, put to use without calculating the social as well as economic consequences that can be at least partially anticipated from that employment of the machine. It is also a moral option to abstain from using the machine. In other realms, that principle has occasionally been applied, notably, of course, in the national policy to circumscribe the testing and use of nuclear weapons. That abstention is justified because of the grotesque threat which nuclear weapons pose to the survival of human life. A similar argument might well be advanced for not utilizing certain technological "advances." Anyway, it should cause men to be morally critical as to what technology might do to the humanity of life.

It is, I suggest, in this realm, more than any other, that the struggle about the idea of American society is being fought, once again, in the present day. For all the public attention given now to the war on poverty and civil rights, at the moment it appears that the institutions of property are prevailing against the rights of human beings.

In any case this is the struggle that will determine whether American society has the moral as well as the technical capability to end poverty.

Chapter Two
The Political Crisis

It has happened to them according to
the true proverb, the dog turns back
to his own vomit.

II Peter 2:22

THE VENERABLE ideological conflict in our society between those who regard property, and the ownership or
management of property, as the moral basis for society
and those persuaded that human rights must have precedence in the ordering of society and the making of public
policy once more dominates the American scene. That is
most obvious in the war on poverty, in popular attitudes
toward money and other forms of property, in uncritical
esteem for technics for their own sake rather than for
the purpose of enhancing human life. An American may
take either side in this ideological conflict, since significant
authority for both can be found in the origins and history
of the American nation.

The differing conceptions of society represented in
these two contesting ideologies do not have specific identi-
fications with either of the surviving major political parties
in America. Although eastern Republicans, for instance,
are commonly stereotyped as Wall Street brokers and
bankers and, hence, associated with the property interests,
some of them have long been constructively associated
with the issues of human rights, particularly with respect
to the survival of political freedom and the attainment of
equal education and business and employment opportunities for Negro citizens. On the other hand, no more zealous
and, indeed, strident advocates of property as the dominant institution of society can be located than the die-hard
segregationists among the southern Democrats.

These ideologies have adherents in both political parties, and the so-called rank and file of both parties seem to
acquire their party affiliations not out of ideological considerations but by inheritance or because of local circumstances (my father first registered as Republican, although
he had no property to speak of, because a friend of his
was running in that party's primary and sought his vote)

or because one party is ascendant in a particular jurisdiction (in New York and Boston, immigrants initially were enrolled by the big-city Democratic machines). I would venture that most ordinary party members barely give a second thought to ideology in relation to their own party affiliation unless or until their own civil rights or property interests are directly threatened.

That neither ideological position can be neatly identified with one party or the other, but each is in conflict within both parties at many echelons, may also indicate that many Americans in both parties regard concern for human rights and property rights as implying views of society which are compatible.

I, for one, believe they *could* be. As a Christian, I am not at all opposed to the private ownership of property, so long as property becomes no yardstick of a person's moral posture. To accumulate or control property is in itself no proof of God's favor or a man's intrinsic superiority over other men; to be bereft of property is no evidence that a man is either abandoned by God or less than another man. Property is no proof of moral excellence; poverty is not morally reprehensible.

Where the two ideologies become incompatible is where, as in the era of chattel slavery, property is accorded such a radical preference over persons as to have an idolatrous status. Where that occurs, the propertyless, the dispossessed, the so-called "minorities," are morally certain to be gravely restricted—if not altogether stifled—in their freedom as human beings. Where that happens, society is apt to become so enamored with the idol of property that it ends up in self-immolation: it worships its own death as a society.

What is distressing in the contemporary eruption of this

struggle is the breakdown in rational public dialogue between the adherents of property and the advocates of human rights. The genius of political democracy is the freedom of public discourse and the open competition of differing opinions, ideas, and interests. Democracy is abused where that does not exist and, I fear, the American democracy is sorely abused today. The explicit confrontations between the opposing views are not only marred by distortion, defamation, and hysterics, but, perhaps unwittingly, the very right to engage in public controversy is being so eroded that it is now doubtful whether it can survive.

Pathology and Politics

Some of the factors which account for the irrationality and, indeed, pathology which characterize the present conflict of property *vs* persons can be identified, particularly in politics.

The most conspicuous and perhaps the most ominous (though by no means the only) instance was in the 1964 Presidential campaign. The image that bore the name of the Republican party in that campaign was not typical of that party and can only be considered as a usurpation of that party as a democratic institution. Even very conservative commentators, like William Buckley, characterized the whole episode as a debacle so far as the conservative cause within the framework of American democracy is concerned.

Although it be assessed as an aberration, it was no mere apparition, stalking the scene for a moment and then disappearing. Despite electoral defeat, the forces and purposes which captured the machinery of the national Republican nominating convention and conducted the campaign are still militant in American society. That makes the 1964 San Francisco convention an event which must not be forgotten but, rather, is to be regarded as an omen for all citizens who care for the survival of democracy in America.

The San Francisco convention was repeatedly characterized by the media covering it as a happening more like a religious revival than a political convention. The sessions were dominated, it was said, by "evangelical fervor" and a "fundamentalist spirit."

Well it might have been, because a real religion *was* revived there, on a scale and with an articulation for which its adherents had long hungered. It is a religion indigenous to America's past. Though reason might conclude that it is a religion irrelevant to the realities of this country in this century, though prudence might counsel that it is suicidal because of its totalitarian tendencies for society, though the zealots of this religion seem to be peculiarly tormented people, common sense argues that this religion cannot be dismissed, since it did in fact dominate the last convention of one of the two major political parties in America, and because it continues to flourish within the precincts of the Republican party. Even Senator Thruston Morton, who presided at the Cow Palace, and Senator Everett Dirksen, who loaned himself for a while to the cause, along with several other national party leaders, now concede the importance of this movement, and have at last announced that the Republican party cannot countenance political totalitarians in its ranks.

Meanwhile, this same religion flourishes on other fronts

and forms, apart from political parties, in churches, parent-teacher organizations, school and library boards, community service organizations, through an estimated seven hundred radio programs and countless other guises. The John Birch Society alone, for example, in 1965 had twice the income of the Republican National Committee.

The credo of this religion, as enunciated at the 1964 convention in a most painstaking form, was expressed in Senator Goldwater's address accepting the nomination. And since Goldwater is given to constantly complaining that what he says is misunderstood, but boasted that his acceptance speech was a model of plain English, it is to that—and not to any of his random, extemporaneous or spontaneous utterings—that one presumably may look to ascertain the dogmatics of the faith which Goldwater bespoke and served while a Presidential candidate. The introit of that authoritative declaration of faith was:

> From this moment, united and determined, we will go forward together dedicated to the ultimate and undeniable greatness of the whole man.

This is not empty rhetoric, for the nominee set forth quite specifically a doctrine of man—one, by the way, which it behooves heretics, as well as the true believers, to understand, since those who are not dedicated to it are guilty not of "mere political differences or mere political mistakes" but of "a fundamentally and absolutely wrong view of man, his nature and his destiny."

What, then, is the anthropology of this religion? Who is this "whole man"? And of what does his "greatness" consist?

The true man is the acquisitive man—a man is whole

if he procures, possesses, and profits from property. The greatness of man is dependent upon "the sanctity of property." Such is the elementary doctrine of this religion that provides the moral criteria by which both men and societies are judged:

> We see in private property and in economy based upon and fostering private property the one way to make government a durable ally of the whole man rather than his determined enemy.

Generically, the doctrine is one of self-justification. A man who wills to do so and who does not suffer the hindrance of government can perfect his own salvation by the getting, holding, and using of private property. Thus salvation is not universal, nor, in *any* sense, by God's election but competitive and comes to the man whose worth and worthiness are proved by the property he controls, earns, or owns. To have property is evidence of moral excellence, defines individual dignity, and is the divine reward for self-reliance. In such a view the failure of a man to acquire property not only aborts his personal fulfillment but must be counted as sin or as the consequence of the interference of evil. If a man has no property he must be wasteful or self-indulgent or slothful or bereft of initiative, or else victim of sinister, ruthless, insatiable, dehumanizing governmental power.

Much worse than such sinners or slaves—who, having little or no property of their own, have neither virtue nor humanity—are those who, having property, are not true believers, do not uphold and propagate this religion, and even pursue and persecute those who do believe. It is not, as the nominee himself indicated, just a matter of differing opinions which might be moderated or tolerated; it is a struggle against sin itself. Sin is to be shunned and sinners cast out. The only reconciliation for the sinner is in his own repentance. That was applied to Governor Scranton, a man of property: when he rose to concede defeat at the convention and recited the traditional overtures for party unity, he had to be repudiated. Though beaten, he vowed to fight again, though meanwhile he promised he would support the ticket. Such an attitude was considered arrogance, not repentance. With it, there can be no compromise without contamination; the only remedy is exorcism. That is why at the convention Governor Rockefeller, also a man of property, could not be heeded, lest the unwary be tempted, nor even heard, lest ears be defiled. Rockefeller would not recant, thus let him suffer humiliation for his apostasy.

Not surprisingly, the doctrine of the acquisitive man as the whole man regards foreign economic aid as squander. Applied specifically to issues of American society, it considers welfare assistance as reward for weakness, social security as surrender of self-reliance, public works as restraints of commerce, Medicare as an invasion of privacy, product quality, packaging, and advertising standards as subversive of a competitive market, the war on poverty as indulgence of sinners, fluoridation as a restraint of choice, and taxation as a necessary—but temporary—evil. Goldwater complained that the incumbent administration had "talked and talked and talked and talked the words of freedom but [had] failed and failed and failed in the works of freedom."

To propagate the works of freedom, so defined, is therefore a divinely commissioned national purpose for America in the world. "The Good Lord raised this mighty

Republic to be a home for the brave and to flourish as the land of the free." While God is said to be "the author of freedom," Americans are freedom's "models" and "missionaries" on earth because they "have earned it." With such a formidable patron as God, nuclear war can be risked on behalf of this conception of freedom. In the name of God, the American mission is to restrain those forces in the world which threaten this idea of freedom. The economic, political, and military activities undertaken in support of such convictions cannot legitimately be considered colonialism, since they are simply a defense of freedom. America's manifest destiny in the cause of this freedom must no longer be compromised or restrained by membership in the United Nations. If the world longs for peace, let peace mean *Pax Americana*.

It is clear that there is nothing novel in this religion or in the application of its doctrine to concrete issues. The danger the 1964 Republican convention dramatized was that, by being vested in a political form, citizens would not recognize it as a religion of fanatical appeal. For the true believers the dispute was not over what is realistic but what is ultimately right; was not concerned with human justice, but with their own justifications; was not about political philosophy but religious truth. In such a cause, there must be no "mistaken humility," the ends authorize any means, and "extremism" in the defense of "freedom" is no vice. The alarm of so many citizens at Senator Goldwater's remarks was based on their assumption that he was speaking politically, whereas the nominee himself remained astonished and angry at the criticism of such statements in his convention address, because he was really talking about his religious commitment.

Throughout the campaign, there were ominous signs of

links between the candidate's adherents and an array of extremists, both political and religious, in this country as well as elsewhere. General Edwin Walker appeared ecstatic that his fellow Episcopalian was nominated. Both ideological and financial backing for Governor Wallace of Alabama, who had his own aspirations, was suddenly and secretly switched to support Senator Goldwater. A man who managed the Robert Welch candidacy for public office in Massachusetts became the chief of campaign operations in New England. Gestures of sympathy were extended to Fascist remnants in Germany. The candidate bragged of his awe of military authority. Radical and long-discredited malcontents among the Protestant sects, like Carl McIntyre, the defrocked Presbyterian fundamentalist, and Billy Hargis and his self-styled Christian anti-Communist crusade, were encouraged. Some who worked openly for Goldwater by day masked in Klan costumes at night. Even Negroes considered "Uncle Toms" by their own people were excluded from political recognition in the party of Abraham Lincoln. Opponents suffered vilification and threats of bodily harm. The nominee himself shunned direct interrogation by the public media. General Eisenhower was treated with a mock deference that bordered on ridicule. Bloodless inquisitions were quietly executed, purging the Republican party of moderates with a long record of loyalty. All these developments were publicly reported and are common knowledge; what more actually happened one fears to conjecture.

Both the ideas and tactics which the candidate advocated are notoriously popular with totalitarian mentalities. For example, it is more effective to have decisions made by the military than to maintain civilian control.

Law and order require the crushing of organized social protest. The path to peace traverses the brink of war. Scapegoats explain whatever is amiss and popularize whatever is to be changed. Simple answers to perplexing issues are what the people want—and all that they deserve. If such views are then criticized in the nation's press, it is because they have been distorted. As for the "moderates," they want harmony so much they are prepared to surrender their principles. Falsehoods repeated often enough will be believed. The way to win is to induce opponents to destroy one another.——The San Francisco Cow Palace rang with echoes from the Munich beer hall.

There is no more cynical example of political ethics in American history than the exploitation in the Goldwater campaign of the racial crisis. While boasting personally of a pure heart, the Senator invoked the Constitution against itself in opposing the Civil Rights Act; simultaneously, it was calculated that an appeal for an end to political debate on civil rights would endear this candidacy to all those white citizens who wish that the Negro revolution had never happened and would somehow just go away. And unless he were a knave or faker, how could Goldwater not have known—as his managers and ghost writers must have known, unless they were fools or racists—that such an appeal was morally certain to encourage a despair among Negro citizens which could have no outlet but violence!

Such traffic in racism, whatever its explanation, did not make Goldwater president of the United States. Indeed, after the implications of his campaign were emphatically pointed out to him—notably in the statement of over nine hundred bishops, clergy, and laity of the Episcopal Church, Goldwater's own denominational affiliation—

the candidate himself began to realize how cruelly he had been manipulated by the very extremists with whom he had sympathized, whom he had sought to defend as enthusiastic patriots, and whose ideas of society he had proclaimed. Goldwater's candidacy legitimately aroused the fears of many who had known totalitarianism in foreign lands. But Goldwater himself exhibited none of the dark genius possessed by Hitler. Nevertheless, for the fanatical religionists who idolize property, and for the wide assortment of racial and political totalitarians who were mobilized by Goldwater's candidacy, the campaign represented a glorious opportunity and an astonishing achievement. Goldwater is not Hitler—no doubt that is why he has been so unceremoniously discarded by the extremists for whom his nomination was a great boon and culmination of a tremendous effort. Yet despite Johnson's landslide victory, the Goldwater candidacy represented a great victory for political extremism because in several areas it brought into ideological association and actual alliance those who worship the "sanctity" of property and those who, for these or other causes, are avowed and militant totalitarians in the United States.

My argument is not that *all* those who esteem property rights as more fundamental in society than human rights are totalitarians, or even that they *all* supported the Goldwater nomination and candidacy. Nor, on the other hand, is it argued that *all* Americans committed to totalitarianism are motivated by idolization of property or even possess much property as such. (Apart from the obvious example of the Communists, many totalitarians in the American Nazi Party, the Minutemen, the John Birch Society, or the Ku Klux Klan would be sociologically classified as poor.) What is asserted is rather that the Goldwater effort provided a catalyst which brought into contagious proximity those who regard property idolatrously and the pathological racists and paramilitarists and Fascists in America. That was the historic accomplishment wrought at the Cow Palace.

The Revenge of the WASP's

What is now needed is some inquiry into the relationship of American white Anglo-Saxon Protestantism to the idolatry of property proper to those fascinated by totalitarian remedies for social problems.

The idolatry of property, of course, is an old religion. It was practiced in medieval feudalism and in the era of colonial empires. It has its American roots in certain forms of Protestantism which developed and flourished among owners of land, holders of slaves, frontier settlers, country people, and pioneer capitalists. If such religion seems simplistic, we should remember that the world appeared smaller then. If this faith is antiquated, remember that it was suited to some of the realities of the late eighteenth and nineteenth centuries in this nation. If, in retrospect, Protestantism is to be criticized for its accommodation to the culture of those times, remember that conformity to the world is still commonplace among those who profess to be Christians, and always remains their most subtle temptation. If times have moved and Americans live now in the twentieth century—whether they find it congenial or not—that does not in itself destroy a religion so convenient to men who judge their own initiative as their moral justification and so reassuring to those white Anglo-Saxons who suppose that God gave them this land as a reward for their enterprise.

The times have changed: The American frontier is no longer a wilderness territory in the West which, despite all its hazards, at least had space in which to live and water to drink and air to breathe. Today the frontiers are the blighted, congested, polluted urban centers, especially in the North, which have become increasingly unfit for human habitation and manifestly incapable of being effectively governed within the inherited city, county, and state jurisdictions. Real property and the production of tangible goods are no longer so important, but one's identity is predicated on the ability to obtain and manipulate credit and to indulge in so-called luxuries that are promoted as status symbols. The very machines which human ingenuity has conceived and constructed turn on men and rob them of jobs—even, it seems, of the labor of thinking for themselves. The affluence of a majority of the American population is—ironically and dangerously —secured by the entrapment in poverty of the remainder. Many Negro citizens have reached the limit of human endurance and are ready to die on the streets of Natchez, Mississippi, or Rochester, New York, rather than suffer a single more assault upon their humanity and their birthright as Americans. The push of a button, in these times, can turn on a light bulb or exterminate mankind. Yet in 1964 a man who inherited a department store ran for president of the United States, extolling initiative and self-reliance in a world in which toilet paper is a luxury most human beings cannot afford to buy.

The times have changed indeed, but American Protestantism has kept the shrine of property, and the doctrine that the acquisitive man is the whole man is still defiantly preached, with only those allowances for change required to maintain property as an idol. How easily, thus, the courage of the pioneer became equated with the guile of the so-called self-made man! How quickly paper replaced land as the symbol of property! How shrewdly has the piety of the settler been attributed to the salesman! Whatever the verdict on this faith in its earlier expressions in previous centuries, it is by such mutations as these that it has managed its survival in this century.

And while this has been the religion harbored by a good many sectarian Protestants, it cannot be dismissed just because it is espoused by extremists, malcontents, and some victims of paranoia. Too many pulpits in mainline Protestant churches have echoed the same idolatry of property and the same teaching of justification by acquisition. How often has the most notorious of Protestant preachers—Norman Vincent Peale—assured his listeners that religion is a business asset because God rewards the man determined to get what he wants! It is no wonder that Dr. Peale's books and sermons are redundant with anecdotes of the uses of "prayer" and "positive thinking" to induce a fierce and persistent pursuit of personal fortune, since he himself is paid as much as $3,000 an appearance to recite these stories, appropriately, at conventions of salesmen and dealers of some of the great business houses.

But Peale is no exception among Protestant preachers. How often have others preached the same lesson—although with less reason, since they are not as grandly compensated—because that is what they sense their people want to hear? Why have so many Protestant congregations forsaken the dispossessed in the cities by literally closing their doors, packing up their possessions, and moving to the suburbs? And why do so many Protestants think that their only involvement with the poor, if any, is a matter of their generosity and charity? Why is so very much of the wealth of the churches invested in merely maintaining churchly institutions? Why has the acquiring and managing of property become the symbol of the "successful" congregation of "respectable" folk? How many Protestants care for the Gospel of visiting prisoners, healing the sick, loving outcasts, and giving all that one possesses to the poor to follow Christ?

This is not to say that Protestantism has been without movements which embodied a protest against perversion of the Gospel in the idolization of property. The social gospel movement, Christian pacifism, the inner-city ministries, the ecumenical dialogue, the involvement of Christians in direct action in the racial crisis—all these have provided reminders of the prophetic spirit. Whatever valid criticisms can be made about any of these forces within Protestantism, they are at least evidence of that compassion for the world and affirmation of the value of human life characteristic of biblical faith. But despite the many Christians—clergymen, theologians, and laymen—whose words and actions have proclaimed the biblical faith, the conclusion seems inescapable that their combined witness has not threatened the conscience of the vast multitude of white Anglo-Saxon Protestants in America. Such voices may even have aroused consternation and a more impetuous allegiance among the idolaters, provoking cruel reprisals, particularly against the clergy.

Those reprisals take many forms. I know one Presbyterian minister who preached a sermon on poverty and the Christian conscience; the next morning, his automobile had been painted red, and his wife began receiving obscene

telephone calls, threatening her children and her own
safety if this "Communist" clergyman did not leave the
community. This happened, by the way, in New York
State, not in Orange County, California, and the culprit
turned out to be a member of the church board. Another
minister, a white man, upon returning from the Selma-
Montgomery March to his Midwestern parish, found himself being accused, in a vestry meeting, of being a Negro.
Apparently the vestryman could find no other explanation
for the minister's action. The great Episcopal Cathedral
in New York—from which location, on Morningside
Heights, one can literally spit down on the Harlem slums
—remains incomplete because episcopal support on behalf of equal rights for all citizens has caused many laymen to cancel pledges and change bequests. A young
priest was forced by his ecclesiastical superiors to leave
his ministry in the tenements and on the streets because he
was becoming "too involved" and was "neglecting" his
duties. Multiply such incidents by the thousand and it may
suggest the extent to which the Gospel is being quite
literally persecuted today by those whose idol is property,
whose religion is now being threatened by the crises of
poverty and race, and whose real god is Death.

In any case, there had been a long preparation for that
great congregation of white Anglo-Saxon Protestants who
gathered at the 1964 Republican convention. Ironically,
the one they had chosen to lead them would not have been
welcome in the America for which they have such nostal-
gia. He was, after all, of Polish immigrant stock; his own
wealth had come by inheritance and marriage; his father
was a Jew; in short, he is no WASP. Yet sometimes
prophets come disguised and, anyway, this one recited
what they had yearned to hear, not just in sanctuaries or

in secret meetings but from the very center stage of the nation.

It would be wrong, however, to despise all those who idolize property as "kooks" or "Neanderthals." Many are, no doubt, solid, well-intentioned, honest, and sincerely—if improvidently—self-righteous folk. If they seem extravagantly uninformed and deeply frustrated, if their views are archaic and sometimes nonsensical, if they become hysterical when they contemplate the Negro citizen as an equal, if they live in fear that the poor will no longer be appeased and might even become free, if they are frantic enough to believe in their viscera that Eisenhower abetted the Communists or that the Warren Court is subversive, it is not necessarily because they are innately sinister, or sick, or insane. Many of these people believe that these times and these issues represent the test of the religious faith which they inherited. If their cherished beliefs do not somehow now prevail, it would mean either that God had abandoned them to *His* own enemies—in which case, there must be no God at all—or else He has long been displeased with their supplications and burnt offerings—in which case their religion is false and their faith in vain. If they do not persist and predominate soon, they will not even possess the solace of being right, though rejected, which has nourished them through long years. If they are not in fact vindicated by their idolatry, it will mean that the ideals to which they have been dedicated are significantly responsible for the conditions they most fear. In other words, what chiefly motivates otherwise respectable citizens to become Birchers and Minutemen is not malice, though there are the malevolent among them, but a sublimated sense of guilt which whispers to them that their own worship of acquisitiveness is somehow the proximate cause of poverty and slums, a provocation of crime in the streets, an incitement to racial disorder, and a major reason why American power is resented abroad. What is at issue for those who value property as an idol is the most traumatic question of all: does the doctrine of man's Fall apply to them, as well as to everyone else?

If for a large number of citizens, particularly WASP's, this is what is at stake in the American social crisis, any extremity can be justified, and abstinence from extremism is morally wrong, precisely, if naïvely, as Senator Goldwater proclaimed.

There is a radical irony in the position, thus, of white Anglo-Saxon Protestants who traditionally have opposed social action by Christians where their apostasy, in the idolatry of property, now results in their intense involvement in action-oriented extremist groups like the John Birch Society.

The Prospects for an American Totalitarianism

There are now said to exist some eighty-seven avowedly totalitarian organizations in the United States. Many are very small and, no doubt, inconsequential, but the most notorious of them—the Birch Society, the Christian Anti-Communist Crusade, the Ku Klux Klan, the Minutemen —spent nearly thirty million dollars in 1965 and their membership ranks are swelling. The Birchers boasted, after the Goldwater defeat, of a huge increase in their rolls. Goldwater did not capture the White House for the totalitarians, but the campaign perhaps accomplished something more significant. It activated them in a way they have not enjoyed previously, and attracted into their ranks a great multitude of new recruits, especially among those for whom property has become an idol. They have been enabled to invade hundreds of precincts of a major party, they exercise control or a balance of power in scores of county committees, and in some states they are represented in the highest party councils. Not content with political infiltration, they have penetrated dozens of reputable community organizations—parent-teacher associations, veterans groups, and civic clubs. They have seized control of vestries, sessions, and boards of many local churches and are frequently encountered trying to curtail, through threats of economic reprisals, the exercise of academic freedom in colleges and universities. They harass editors and often have control of the advertising revenue to enforce their wishes. Their views gain currency far beyond the immediate borders of their own constituencies.

High officials, notably among the professional police authorities, are frequently heard echoing sentiments most appealing to the totalitarian mentality. C. D. DeLoach, associate director of the F.B.I., for example, finds a common denominator between civil rights demonstrators, the peace movement, and student protests and "racketeers, Communists, narcotics peddlers, filth merchants and others of their ilk [who] hold themselves above the law." A former police commissioner in New York City while in office made it a matter of administrative policy in the department not to advise an apprehended person of his constitutional rights on the grounds that this impeded police work. One consequence of that policy was later exposed in the celebrated Whitmore case, in which a young Negro was brutally coerced into confessing to two abominable sex crimes he did not commit.

There are those who fear that the American democracy is threatened chiefly by the extraordinary power concentrated in the Pentagon and who wonder whether the movie, *Dr. Strangelove,* is really so fanciful as it at first seems. Others fear that the Republican party will be so deeply subverted by the John Birch Society that its demise as a democratic political party will be the precursor of an American totalitarianism. Although I remain, for the time being, a registered Democrat, I think a forceful argument can be made for becoming a Republican, active at the ward and precinct level in order to fight the totalitarians at the point of their initial infiltration in politics. There are battles to be fought on many fronts and there are a multitude of reasons to be wary about the future of democracy in America.

My own concern, however, is the changing role of the police in our society as it steadily assumes a specifically military function. The breakdown in public confidence in the police to acquit their duties without prejudice to the rights of citizens, especially among the people of the ghettos, has already been discussed. There is now deep misgiving about the police not only among those in the ghetto but among others who, though never victims of police abuse themselves, were as profoundly shocked by police action during the Harlem riots in 1964 and the Watts riots of 1965 as they were on the day the posse charged and whipped and gassed the Selma marchers.

In such a context, virtually any action by the police invites suspicion—even reckless and false accusations of police brutality or other abuse are apt to be believed. From that point of view alone, the police themselves should welcome the establishment of a bona fide civilian complaint review board in every major city. At the same time, I am aware that many white citizens, insulated from the realities of ghetto life, living in almost total segregation from the people of the ghetto, deprived of any human contact with Negro or Puerto Rican citizens, enamored with prejudicial stereotypes of the poor, apathetic toward the civil rights movement, and fearful of any significant social change, think that the remedy for unrest in society is more police. In most great cities "crime in the streets" has been seized upon as a political issue by candidates looking for easy popularity; and escalating the police presence in the city seems both a practical and righteous solution to prosperous white property owners.

But such an approach to our established disorder would be courting calamity. In other words, the real peril now is that the response of the public authorities to social protest—symbolized most poignantly and urgently by the legitimate discontent of the ghetto people—is to seal it off (since it can no longer be hidden), contain it, and then suppress it ruthlessly. The mentality that governs the reaction of police headquarters to the ghetto riots of 1964 and 1965 is that of an occupation army. Indeed, a police training manual used in some of the larger Northern cities reads very much like the training manual which indoctrinated those of us who served in the military occupation in Germany in the postwar period. Not only in the hinterlands of Alabama and Mississippi, but right in the heartland of American urban society, the imminent danger to the constitutional fabric of this country is that the police, in response to movements of protest, will be unwittingly transformed into a military organization, accountable only to itself. If that happens, all citizens, not just those of the ghetto, will live as an "occupied people," and the idea of an American totalitarianism will no longer be remote.

The Protest Movements

The tendency toward the militarization of the police and the public acceptance of such a change in the social function of the police have become aggravated recently by the emergence of protest movements in realms other than civil rights, notably in the organized demonstrations against the American military involvement in Vietnam.

One sign of this emerging tendency is the readiness with which the public mind has come to associate demonstrations with violence. The day after a parade in New York City (October 16, 1965), organized by some of the peace groups, a reporter in an interview asked me: "What did you think of the riots yesterday?" The answer, of course, was "What riots?" There had been no riots; there had been a peaceful procession of some 15,000 citizens down Fifth Avenue. The sponsors of the demonstration had obtained a police permit. There was no riot nor any incident of violence whatsoever, but in the mind of this reporter, presumably a relatively well-informed person, demonstrations of protest were not to be distinguished from rioting. If such a failure to discriminate is widespread—and I fear it is—it means that the public mind has become more and more receptive to the militarization of the police at the same time that the police increasingly regard their functions and prerogatives in a military fashion.

In addition, the editorial reaction to the peace movement in general, and to the anti-Vietnam war protests in particular, has, for the most part, characterized those in protest as unwashed, draft-dodging, freeloving, hapless beatniks. As if they were cuss words, the names "peacenik" and "Vietnik" have been coined. In truth, some very responsible and venerable American citizens have been leading these protests. Dorothy Day, A. J. Muste, Norman Thomas, Dr. Benjamin Spock, Norman Cousins, Rabbi Abraham Heschel, Father Daniel Berrigan, Bishop William Crittenden, can hardly be described as beatniks. More than a score of the senators and a hundred or more of their colleagues in the House of Representatives who have raised similar questions about the American military involvement in Vietnam can hardly be characterized in such fashion either. The *Washington Post,* in its edition of November 27, 1965, carried a cartoon depicting the antiwar demonstrators as beatniks, but, significantly, its front-page article on the March on Washington, which had taken place that day, presented contradictory evidence. In that article the newspaperman who had witnessed the march reported, almost regretfully, that most of the marchers were in fact middle-aged, middle-class, and that most of the younger people appeared to be neatly attired, clean-cut, earnest college students.

Nevertheless the impression remains, I am afraid, in the minds of most citizens that demonstrations mean riots and that those who demonstrate thereby impugn their own loyalty, where, in truth, they manifest their profound allegiance to the ethics of democracy. One congressman prepared a resolution that would make protests against the Vietnam war acts of treason. So harsh and hysterical has been the editorial and public reaction to the peace demonstrations that some civil rights leaders have been counseling the civil rights movement to abandon further marches or similar tactics lest the hostility to the peace movement tarnish the civil rights cause. The atmosphere of hysteria has even led the Georgia State Assembly to refuse to seat Julian Bond, a legally elected Negro representative from

Atlanta, because he supported a statement of the Student
Nonviolent Coordinating Committee criticizing American
military involvement in Vietnam.

What is happening in all this is the erosion, if not yet
the uprooting, of the right to dissent. The issue is most
acute in the realm of foreign military policy. The last
great, free, open-ended, democratic public debate on foreign policy in this country was the isolationist debate in
the years prior to the American entrance into the Second
World War. During the war the principle of bipartisanship
was established, and I, for one, do not wish to dispute its
justification during so momentous a crisis as that war was.
But since that war the principle has been extended to
accomplish, for all practical purposes, a cloture of public
discussion about foreign policy and, with but few exceptions, to prevent debate in the Congress as well. Bipartisanship in foreign military policy has reached its most danger-
ous sophistication in the rubric of consensus enunciated
in the Johnson administration. It is only one further step
to abrogate the right of dissent in this society. Senator
William Fulbright, among a host of other distinguished
and informed senators who are neither beatniks nor raving
radicals, has had the political courage to expose this peril
to American democracy, and the televised hearings in
the spring of 1966 of the Senate Foreign Relations Committee was a major reassertion of the American tradition.
It is true that President Johnson has given at least lip
service to the idea that the right to protest must be hon-
ored, but these assertions have to be weighed against the
enormous pressures to conformity constantly exercised by
the White House. And national temper on political dissent
in the area of foreign policy can also be measured by the
efforts of labor unions to quash public protests, as in di-

minishing the impact of a march by limiting its size through the refusal of unionized bus drivers to transport marchers.

Moreover, it seems to me that every possible impediment is being placed in the way of a full, honest, and free Senate debate on Vietnam, including the denial of senatorial access to critical witnesses and the usurpation of public attention by the administration.

The erosion of the right of dissent with respect to foreign military policy, which has taken place under the apparently benign principle of bipartisanship since the end of the Second World War, means that there is now one generation of Americans of voting age who have never experienced the vigor of free public debate in this realm and who are quite unaccustomed to the practice of democracy, that is, to informing themselves critically, and to questioning prevailing policy. That is why I am grateful for *every* movement of protest which has a serious purpose, whether I happen to concur with a particular protest or not. The only way the right of dissent can be maintained in the American democracy is in its exercise. If a distinct minority in the colonies had not dissented, there would be no American democracy, for a majority of the colonists opposed the Revolution.

The Immolation of Americans

The right to protest has taken many forms in American history, but recently in this country there have been several instances of self-immolation—events for which we seem to have no precedent. Five citizens of the United States have—so far—committed suicide by burning their own bodies. Another has recovered, insofar as that is possible, from a clumsy attempt to perform the same act. Whether these examples will be further imitated by the time this is published is difficult to predict.

It is worth recalling that in 1963, at least twelve monks of the zealous political sects of Buddhism in Vietnam died of self-immolation in protest against the corruption, banality, and brutality of the regime of Ngo Dinh Diem. It is also worth remembering that this regime was installed, and for a long time subsidized and sanctioned, by the American government.

Despite the difficulty of making estimates on such matters, I do not recollect that at the time the Buddhist immolations had much impact, one way or the other, upon the sympathies of the American people. There were, of course, those ghastly technicolor photographs in *Life* of some of the burnings, but I suspect that they were no more offensive to the sensibilities of most Americans than, say, the lurid technicolor pictures of intestinal surgery which the same periodical has also published. Gory sights do not excite the American conscience.

Besides, the Buddhist immolations happened when Vietnam seemed much farther away than it now does and Americans were even more desperately ignorant about that beleaguered country than they are today. The Buddhist "barbecues"—as Madame Nhu styled them—could be dismissed with facility by Americans as religious and political fanaticism—the sort of thing which is apt to happen in foreign and unsophisticated places with strange and unpronounceable names.

Actually there is ample evidence, as I learned in Vietnam, that the Buddhist burnings were actions chosen on the basis of a sophisticated ethical and tactical protest,

aimed at dramatizing the intolerability of the Diem dicta-
torship. So far as the majority of the South Vietnamese
were concerned, this had been government by terrorism,
torture, and mayhem, and, so far as the American presence
in South Vietnam mattered, by manipulation, guile, and
obsequiousness.

The immolations were not impetuous acts but care-
fully staged events; those willing to be burned alive first
volunteered, and then some were selected by their peers.
Those selected endured pious preparations for their witness in prayer and fasting; they were administered medica-
tion to mitigate their agony; and, while burning, they were
usually, though not always successfully, shielded by their
brothers from the interference of authorities or onlookers
who might interrupt or halt the ritual. In death, the ashes
of flesh and bones were carried in procession through the
streets and accorded homage in the temples.

The Buddhist sectarians who advocated and practiced
immolation as a form of profound social protest in 1963
are said to hold religion and politics to be so intermingled
as to be indistinguishable. If their actions are to be regarded as extraordinarily extremist by Americans, it must
at least be said of them that they fanaticized their patriot-
ism. There are, after all, many in the United States who
esteem *that* as the highest civic virtue, although they are
for the most part Birchers and not Buddhists.

From this distance, it appears that the Buddhist immolations were instances of authentic martyrdom, not in
the particular sense in which that word is occasionally used
in the New Testament and in the subsequent history of
the Gospel in the world to refer to some Christian who is
put to death by others because he is a Christian, but in the
other, ordinary, sense of a life which is surrendered to

death in adherence to a cause thought to be of greater moral significance than the life sacrificed. Men may dispute about which causes have a dignity that rationalizes such martyrdom, but in the end this remains in the solitary discretion of the martyred, and nobody else at all has any basis by which to judge such commitment unto death.

What can be said, however, of these American immolations?

Buddhist fanatics in faraway places may burn themselves, but there seems something alien, peculiar, and, indeed, inherently unpatriotic in the self-immolation of an American citizen. But this does not mean that these American examples do not have something important to bespeak. Even if Americans can somehow be pardoned by other human beings for moral indifference to the Buddhist martyrs and the protest against American policy implicit in the Buddhist burnings, these American "barbecues" must not be dismissed too casually.

The impulse has been to explain them away as pathetic, precipitous, private acts, having no significance as social protest.

Thus, from the White House itself, the morning after the Quaker Norman Morrison had set himself ablaze outside the Pentagon, came the gratuitous suggestion that Morrison harbored a morbid personal death wish and had utilized the Vietnam war as an excuse to act out his pathological compulsion to suicide. Surely no citizen would dissent so profoundly from American policy as to burn himself to death right outside Secretary McNamara's window; *ergo,* Morrison must have been insane. Conceivably, Norman Morrison was insane; I do not know. For that matter, neither does anyone else, least of all anyone in the White House or any robots in the Pentagon or any propagandists in the State Department. It remains, however, a far more plausible explanation of Morrison's death that he wanted to surrender his life for a cause which he regarded as of greater moral significance than his own life. He had, after all, for a long time been involved in other protests against the American military involvement in Vietnam, and it argues against the notion that his was some grisly personal act that he selected an hour and a location for his immolation certain to attract attention. Maybe Morrison was insane, but it is much more likely that he was, in the same sense as the Buddhists, a martyr.

Much the same thing can be affirmed, I think, about the earliest known American immolation, even though it was not widely publicized nor regarded as of much social significance at the time it took place, March 16, 1965, on a street corner in Detroit. In that first immolation an old woman—eighty-two years of age, Alice Herz by name—ignited herself in protest against the war in Vietnam. She lingered for ten days in agony before she died. In moments of awful lucidity during those days she said that her purpose was not to document "despair but faith in the human spirit." It could, of course, be easily rationalized that such an old woman was near death, anyway, and that her immolation was, as the authorities at the White House said of Morrison, not a social protest but a pathological act accounted for in merely personal terms. The record, however, does not support such an easy excuse, because Alice Herz had long been active in other forms of protest, especially about the Vietnam calamity, and, as with Morrison, her decision to burn herself took place in public and was calculated to be and to become a public protest.

In other words, the pathology most evident in the episodes of Alice Herz and Norman Morrison is not that of these immolations themselves—it appears that they both volunteered for martyrdom—but rather that of a nation which can understand radical dissent only as a sickness, and which so eagerly believes and so pathetically wants to believe that martyrdom is treason.

Yet if Norman Morrison and Alice Herz be counted as political martyrs, this does not mean that the same can be said of the other immolations of Americans. Reliable information is very limited, but, as to the abortive attempt of the woman in South Bend, who survived, and as to the college girl who doused herself with gasoline and succeeded in dying, and as to the Baltimore man who burned himself to death, it seems that all of these were impetuous personal acts. None of these people is known to have been involved in any intentional protest movement about Vietnam or anything else. All suffered individual tragedies of sufficient magnitude to court suicide anyway. None of these incidents took place in any place or at any time premeditated to arouse public notice or to point to issues beyond their personal desperation. The woman who survived was a mother, deeply despondent over the accidental death of her baby. In the instance of the coed, the girl confessed as she died that her act was "because of a personal thing"—apparently her estrangement from a boy—and "had nothing to do with the world situation or Vietnam." In the third case, a man discharged from a mental institution only shortly before, ignited himself and died, leaving a note indicating radical personal motivation for taking his own life. From the meager details available, these appear to have been instances of attempted suicide and of suicide in an ordinary sense, if any attempt at suicide or any suicide can be termed "ordinary." These burnings seem not to have been related to each other, or to the Buddhist immolations, or to the Morrison and Herz witnesses, except insofar as the idea of such a form of death may have been planted in the minds of others (God knows how many others) by the martyrs, both Buddhist and American, and in some of these minds the idea fermented.

The immolation of Roger Laporte, the boy who said he was protesting all the hate in the world, can, I think, be distinguished from each of the other American immolations, as well as from the Buddhist happenings. I knew Laporte and we had talked occasionally about this world in which he beheld and abhorred so much hate. He was not insane, but he was troubled and concerned, as any truly sane man is. He was not conformed enough to have become, like so many of his elders, either a cynic or, what is even worse and even more common, addicted to boredom. He was only twenty-two, but he was not so naïve as to suppose that his death in this fashion would expiate the world of hate. He was a Catholic and he knew that Christians, though they often be persecuted and tortured in this world, do not seek suffering. He was not a martyr (in that ordinary sense) for some cause he thought more important than his own life.

With Roger—this is what I now intuit—it is rather that in the moment in which he ignited his own body he was afflicted with that appalling despair which has concluded that death is the ultimate meaning of existence and that only in the offering of his life to death would his life have significance. A man so fearfully offended by all the hate militant in this world, a man who despairs of any hope this side of death, still nurses a certain vanity that there is one thing which he can do to render his existence morally significant—he can kill himself. Such profound despair is, in fact, an idolatry of the power of death, a way, as it is said biblically, of cursing God.

Yet, as is well known from a great host of witnesses— Job and Peter and Paul and Augustine and Kierkegaard and so many others—it is only from within the very depths of Hell that life is sanctified.

It is affirmed that in the hours in which Laporte lingered in agony he was emancipated from this despair. I believe that to be true with absolute certainty, because it is the absolution of men from the worship of death which is precisely the meaning for men of the Resurrection of Christ.

Indifference as Immolation

In matters such as these—in the Buddhist and, now, the American immolations—the truth of what has happened will not be fully acquainted to men until the Last Day of the world, to the embarrassment and consternation, no doubt, of every single man and, also without doubt, to that subtle amusement with which God practices forgiveness.

Meanwhile, let Americans pay attention to the irony of these immolations. Let it be remembered how few there were who were distressed or moved in any way at what they considered the spectacle of a few odd monks roasting themselves in the streets of Saigon. Recalling that, let it be no surprise at all that when some Americans—for whatever reasons—set themselves afire, there were very few who wept, very few who mourned, very few, in fact, who cared enough for any human life—even their own—to pause long enough to ask why.

That so few Americans lamented the immolations is, I fear, because there are so many Americans who know secretly the harshness with which any inquiry into why these things happen among us must be answered.

Americans cannot bear to question something like these immolations of their fellow citizens or of those foreign monks, because that would risk exposure of the truth that this becomes a society so self-indulgent and so arrogant, so given to idolatry and so decadent, so beguiled with legends, sometimes false, of its own past, and so incapacitated to be self-critical that it can neither admit nor administer to its own most desperate needs for social renewal and reconstruction. Indeed, it becomes a society so pressed—on so many fronts, internally and externally—for its very survival that it seems increasingly bent upon managing to survive by renouncing the very idea of society which is most worthy of survival: that is, persons are more important than property, and in the ordering of communities and nations in this world, the gift of human life itself must have precedence over *all* else.

Americans cannot question these personal immolations; Americans dare not often ask many questions at all any more, because that would expose the truth that this becomes a nation so very fond of death, in ways which permeate its whole public fabric, that it is a society itself engaged in self-immolation.

Chapter Three

The Warfare Between the Races

Lest you be wise in your own conceits, I want you to understand this mystery, brethren: a hardening has come upon part of Israel, until the full number of the Gentiles come in, and so all Israel will be saved.

Romans 11:25

FOR THOSE with hearty appetites for violence it is no longer necessary to stay awake half the night watching late, late shows on television. Nowadays one only has to tune in a newscast to see the sights and hear the sounds of violence in American society.

There is sufficient variety to satisfy every taste or proclivity, and for those who prefer a less vicarious violence than the news of the day offers, more direct exposure and excitement are readily available.

For example, one might want to spend the January or spring collegiate holidays at some beach where students congregate to riot, or, later in the season go to Newport for all the jazz.

Governor Wallace of Alabama, who is no novice about violence, has recommended a ride on a Philadelphia subway, since, should you not witness an assault or have the fortune to be attacked, there is at least the chance of being bitten by a police dog.

According to the *New York Daily News,* which also betrays an affection for violence, those who would prefer their action aboveground should take a stroll in Central Park at night.

Italian-Americans can seek membership in the Mafia, while white Gentile Protestants, as usual, have the most options, since they are eligible for the American Nazi Party, the Minutemen, the Ku Klux Klan, and the John Birch Society.

With the right connections, in certain localities, careers in violence are apparently still possible in the Teamsters Union.

Those who would be victims rather than aggressors need only burn their draft cards.

The young and hardy can enlist in the Marines and, with any sort of luck, end up in Vietnam.

As perhaps a final resort, one can become a cop and seek assignment to occupation duty in one of the black ghettos of the urban North.

All this, of course, is only a way of saying that violence is manifold and commonplace in American society. It seems always to have been so: in the Colonial protests for fair taxation and political independence and in the Revolution itself; in the Indian wars and the conquest of the frontier; in the war between the states and the trauma of the Reconstruction crisis; in the emergence of the labor union movement and in the era of prohibition—to mention but a handful of historical examples—as well as in the present day.

Whether violence is more widespread today than in earlier times I seriously doubt, but how could any accurate measurement possibly be made? Whether there is a pattern of violence peculiar to our time which did not previously exist, I equally doubt—probably no one really knows. Whether the violence modern society suffers is more vehement than in other periods is impossible to assess.

What *is* most significantly different today is that communications are virtually instantaneous: the whole country watched Ruby shoot Oswald. The impact of the incidents and images of violence is immediate upon the consciousness, if not always upon the consciences, of citizens: everyone saw the troopers savagely charge, then lash and gas and stomp the Selma marchers on "Black Sunday" in March of 1965; all knew immediately when and how and who murdered Jonathan Daniels; the Watts riot kept millions watching their TV sets. What *is* different now is that the facts of violence cannot be ignored, or rationalized, or suppressed, or even distorted too much, because there are so many onlookers to every violence.

That makes it difficult to account—in a *rational* way—
for the popularity, especially among the white middle
classes in both North and South, of the falsehood which
equates civil rights demonstrations with violence in the
streets.

One recalls, however, that this mistaken notion has had
faint echoes from ordinarily responsible quarters, notably
in statements of former President Truman ridiculing civil
rights demonstrations such as the Selma march, and in
some of the general lamentations of former President
Eisenhower about the disruption of law and order. Before
that, however, the alleged equation of civil rights protests
and violence gained notorious currency in the 1964 Presidential campaign. Indeed, this propaganda became so
abrasive and blatantly exploitive that Senator Goldwater
himself was moved to repudiate some of this campaign
material as "racist." That repudiation has not, of course,
prevented others, most notably the John Birchers, from
persevering in the same savage lie. The truth, however, is
that violence initiated by Negro and other citizens in the
civil rights movement has been rare and minimal—so
far—especially so if the scope, duration, and depth of the
protests are taken into account. The overwhelming number
of acts of violence in the American racial crisis has been
instigated and executed by white people; their murders,
tortures, mutilations, and bombings of Negroes have almost always been perpetrated with impunity, if not actually accomplished, either directly or collusively, by the
police authorities themselves. (From 1954 through the end
of 1965, there have been sixty-one homicides directly related to civil rights, as to which there has yet to be a single
conviction for murder or manslaughter. It is not possible
to ascertain how many other homicides have been com-

mitted which have never even been reported on a police blotter.) No plaintive rationalizations can erase that dismal record; no amount of whitewash can conceal that much blood.

A Violence of Despair

The violence that *has* erupted in which Negroes have taken the initiative—so far—has been in the riots and skirmishes in the ghettos of Northern cities. It is hard to determine what degree of violence is necessary to have classification as a riot, but by my own calculation, there have been seventeen ghetto riots in 1964 and 1965.

Whatever the computation, these incidents have not been—so far—associated with any civil rights demonstrations as such. There remains an urgent need for an objective inquiry into the causes of the riots. They cannot fairly be blamed upon Negro civil rights leaders. In fact, Negro civil rights leaders have done much more than any others, both to curtail the riots and to work on the scene inside the ghettos after the riots have been quelled. Bayard Rustin dissuaded some in the Harlem riots from exploding a cache of dynamite that was capable of obliterating an entire city block; Dick Gregory was wounded while pleading for a halt to the rioting in Watts. The Southern Christian Leadership Conference has established a beachhead in Chicago's black belt, and the Northern Student Movement has been working for months in several Eastern cities to forestall or ameliorate riot-prone tensions. The Negro civil rights leaders who have been committed for so long to the ethics and tactics of nonviolence recognize, of course, that the riots immediately pose a threat to their philosophy and strategy of social change. They also realize—what apparently most white people cannot comprehend—that nonviolence can prevail in the Negro revolution only if it yields significant results.

Perhaps Malcolm X, the assassinated leader of the Black Muslims, knew this truth better than anyone. He was much misunderstood and editorially maligned as an advocate of violence. That is not true. He doubted that passive resistance would bring substantive progress, foreseeing that it might evoke a greater recalcitrance toward change among the whites. In the face of that prospect, he did *not* advocate aggressive violence by Negroes against white society, but he did uphold the conviction that when a man is assaulted he has the dignity and right to defend himself—one of the most venerable principles of Anglo-Saxon common law.

I am an Episcopalian, not a Quaker. Although (I trust) a peaceful man, I am not an ideological pacifist. I do not assume that all violence is the same, or that every incident of violence is to be uncritically deplored, or that one may never revolt, or that a Christian may never be found in violence. Most likely, the American democracy could not have been constituted in the first place without the Revolution, and nowhere in the world has it been easy to overthrow colonialism without violence. The conscience of Bonhoeffer involved him in a conspiracy to assassinate the head of state in his country—Adolph Hitler—and both in His life and in His death Jesus Christ was not a stranger to violence. At least this should suggest that there are different sorts of violence.

No attempt is made here at any exhaustive or definitive analysis of the ethics of violence, but the history of American social protest teaches us that an important distinction exists between intentional, deliberate, tactical violence, on one hand, and unpremeditated, spontaneous, sporadic violence, on the other. For example, in the early part of the labor revolution, especially in the 1920's, both those in protest and those defending the status quo engaged in willful violence as a means of pursuing their respective social aims. For both sides, violence became integral to strategy and was thought to be the necessary and effective way of achieving certain objectives. The Northern ghetto riots of the 60's represent a very different kind of violence; they have not been premeditated acts, but have incarnated a violence of despair.

They represent a spontaneous violence. Nobody planned or plotted these riots; no one conspired beforehand; no one calculated that such violence would gain anything for anybody. They were *not* the work—as the F.B.I. itself has repeatedly confessed—of professional agitators, disgruntled beatniks, adolescent hoodlums, black supremists, or Communists—though, once the fires of revolt were ignited, it would have been astonishing indeed if some attempts were not made to feed the flames.

It is also significant that, up to now, the violence of the ghetto riots has been internalized. What happened took place inside the ghettos and did not represent a direct assault upon white society or white property or white people. In this sense, the riots have been a symbolic violence. The day when the despair of ghettoized Negro citizens turns into wrath will be the day that someone tries to blow up City Hall or burn down a "white" department store or sabotage an urban rapid transit system. That will be the day when the violence of despair is no longer internalized and confined inside the ghettos but becomes open insurrection against white society.

Almost all the riots—so far—have been occasioned by comparatively trivial and superficially unrelated provocations. The two exceptions are in Chicago and New York. In Chicago, in the summer of 1965, a Negro woman was fatally injured by a fire truck being operated in a grossly negligent manner (there was no driver for the rear-ladder apparatus). In New York, in the summer of 1964, a Negro boy was shot and killed in the presence of scores of other school children by an off-duty white policeman, in circumstances which, to say the very least, were extremely ambiguous. In both these cases, there had been serious incidents: human beings had been either mortally injured or killed.

In the other cases, however—in Trenton, New Jersey, Springfield, Massachusetts, in Watts in Los Angeles—the occasions for riot were relatively inconsequential and, in some cases, actually innocuous. In Rochester, New York, for example, a man and his wife, evidently drunk, were arguing with each other on the sidewalk and were properly arrested for disorderly conduct by the police. In Philadelphia, there was an ordinary traffic violation, and the arresting officer was a Negro. Such common and apparently insignificant incidents were enough, nevertheless, to kindle into riot the accumulated and inherited passions, frustrations, hostilities, grievances, hurts, and pains of an imprisoned people.

In other words, these Northern city riots are a most radical form of violence, perhaps the most volatile there can be: unpremeditated, unpredictable, without tactical goals, undisciplined, chaotic, without focus or definite purpose, a spontaneous combustion of fury. That is the mood which now threatens to overwhelm the civil rights movement.

Despair is probably the most pathetic human response of all, because it operates on the assumption that there is no honest hope of meaningful change. How can we ask the Negro poor to believe that their everyday lives are about to be transformed and that their fragile dreams will not again be shattered? Despair in the ghettos can no longer be appeased by promises and pronouncements about gradual improvements. Despair expresses the defeat of human expectations for society: now that it has been unleashed, it will not be easily or quickly distracted (not even by war), much less deterred or displaced.

The Efficacy of Apathy

The despair which spawns the violence of the American ghettos is nourished as much by the apathy of white society as by the abominable conditions of ghetto existence. The despair of urban Negro citizens is as profound as the apathy of white citizens is obstinate.

No more appropriate symbols of the apathy of the American white establishment exist than in the incumbent political administrations of the principal Northern cities. Warned of impending trouble in Watts in the spring of 1965, Mayor Yorty of Los Angeles refused assistance from federal trouble shooters, which had been offered by representatives of the war on poverty. Mayor Daley, shortly before the first Chicago riot in 1964, publicly boasted that there were no ghettos in Chicago. In Boston a militant racist, Mrs. Louise Hicks, has fashioned a promising political career by her skillful manipulation of the apathy and latent racism of white parents, thereby entrenching her personal power in the school committee and evidencing her availability for the mayoralty office.

Equally typical was the response of Mayor Wagner of New York to the Harlem riots of the summer of 1964. After that trouble had been ruthlessly suppressed by the police, the Mayor called a press conference at which he stated that the unrest in Harlem had some connection with the conditions in which the people there lived from day to day. He mentioned the decrepit, rat-infested tenements, the obsolete, academically inferior schools, the shortage of jobs, the absence of equal opportunity; he even suggested that something should be done. At the end of his administration a year and a half later, however, nothing had been done—categorically and literally, *nothing*. In this respect New York is not unique among the great cities of the nation, but it represents the epitome of white apathy.

If the promises of white people are regarded by Negro citizens as not only empty but perhaps calculated deceptions, and if the white mayors and other public representatives are thought to be somewhat shrewd, if not very subtle cynics, more than any other single thing it is the complacency of white society and the City Halls they still dominate which is responsible. For the secret premise, the hidden assumption, the unstated commitment, the unconscious sentiment of most earnest, well-intentioned, law-abiding, churchgoing, peace-loving, "moderate" white citizens is that the circumstances of life within the black ghettos should be improved, somehow, but that the ghettoization of society will indefinitely remain.

Most white citizens are, as yet, not pathological in their attitudes toward Negroes. They are not vulgar and vicious racists, but they have been reared in an ethos of white supremacy for so long that ghettoization is assumed as normative. They have the idea that the racial unrest in society is due to an insufficient degree of white paternalism, not yet realizing that paternalism is itself a form of racism. What most whites who are not militant racists envision when they hear the words "integration" or "civil rights" is a time when a significant empirical betterment of places like Harlem and Woodlawn and Watts will have been achieved. They entertain images of black ghettos becoming decent and pleasant habitations. What white "moderates" do not realize is that they themselves are ghettoized, not only racially but physically, in the places where they live and study and work and play and worship, and also in their minds and mentalities—and, hence, in their morality.

White "moderates" are still enamored with the possibility of a society in which there is equality but separation, not understanding that equality is inherently incompatible with the radical division of society by race in the basic spheres of life, and that it represents an inequality suffered on both sides of the racial barrier. Whites who fondly assume that "Negroes prefer to live with their own kind" must face the fact that it will only be when Negro citizens have free access to reside and work and study and vote and live wherever they please that such a proposition can be seriously tested. What incites despair inside the black slums is, manifestly, the failure to remedy glaring inequities in housing, education, and employment. Part of the secret of such despair is found in the profound psychological, emotional, and moral insularity of white people who complacently assume that such places as Harlem—even if sometime somewhat improved—will continue to be ghettos.

Indeed, the atrocities of white racists in the Deep South are probably easier to bear than the recalcitrance and ingenuity of white paternalism in the urban North. This accounts in part for the strong reaction within the Negro community to the celebrated Moynihan Report, which had been advanced as the basis for deliberations at the 1966 White House Conference on Civil Rights, and was properly controverted by Dr. Benjamin F. Payton, now Executive Director, Commission on Religion and Race, National Council of Churches. The Moynihan Report, prepared by Daniel P. Moynihan while he was Assistant Secretary of Labor (1963–1965), argues that the legal barriers to the assimilation of Negro citizens have been substantially removed but that the critical obstacle that remains to integration is the breakdown of the Negro family structure and the emasculation of the American Negro male.

Such a position is not exactly untrue, but it is terribly incomplete and misleading unless placed alongside other important factors. The Moynihan Report uncritically assumes that the inherited white family institution and the patterns of assimilation applicable to white immigrants are the criteria of social stability which should and can overcome the disintegration of Negro family life, without acknowledging inherent strengths in the Negro family. Though Moynihan himself is obviously no racist and is a strong advocate of an immediate policy of total employment, his report inadvertently furnishes a subtle rationale for the continuance of white paternalism. It represents a half-truth because it fails to take note of the decadence of the American white family as it may causally relate to the plight of the American Negro family, or as an appropriate standard for a socially mature family structure as such. Of course, if a Moynihan-type report were written—as it well could be—on the parallel breakdown in the white family structure in America and its accompanying defeminization of the white female, it is unlikely that the White House would convene a national conference. But in any case, the racial ghettoization of society will only be more cruelly entrenched by any efforts to make Negro families into facsimile white families.

What is needed to absolve despair is the determination that there be an end to ghettos: every ghetto which blights every city and town in this land with a Negro population must be erased. Only by beginning with that commitment—and there are few signs that white citizens are even contemplating such a commitment—is there a serious possibility of conceiving and executing public policies which can, at once, free the prisoners of the black ghettos and emancipate white Americans from the ghetto of their own complacency.

The ghettos must go; both white and black must be freed from their imprisonments. But what does that imply in terms of concrete public policies? While I have no panaceas, the most significant change would be a conversion in the mentalities of both white and Negro citizens. As for a black ghetto like Harlem, it is now so congested, so deteriorated, and so insufferable as to be mostly beyond rehabilitation—a place unfit for human habitation. But to destroy the Harlem ghetto, rather than futilely to patch it up, would mean that the existing population of Harlem would have to be dispersed and relocated elsewhere in the city, and, more than likely in the suburbs, in localities where from the outset of the dispersion there would have to be integrated housing, education, and employment opportunities.

Legitimate questions could be asked, of course, about whether society has the right to uproot people from where they now live and relocate them somewhere else, but it seems that this is the practical reality wherever citizens are consigned to places like Harlem. No doubt white neighborhoods and schools and businesses in communities where dispersed Negroes arrived would find many patterns of society threatened or changed in such a process, but the answer to that is that the bourgeois white ghettos must also be erased if this is to be an integrated—or simply a human—society.

Perhaps dispersion is not an appropriate remedy, but it is an imaginable step and one that could be undertaken. In fact, it is the sort of policy that might well be considered if the moral commitment of this society became one of abolishing the ghettos instead of merely, at best, preserving and improving them. The important thing is that integration means the disruption and rejection of much that has been taken for granted for many generations in America—a drastic reappraisal of values which has not yet been even theoretically contemplated.

The White Supremist Syndrome

While I mean to furnish no comfort whatever to the pathological racists among white Americans—to those of the Ku Klux Klan or the John Birch Society or others whose reason has been perverted—let it be nevertheless confessed that there is no serious ethical distinction between such racism and the more benign and more secretive white supremacy so common among the great multitudes of "moderate" middle-class whites. No doubt there are aesthetic differences: a Mayor Daley or a Mayor Yorty is not as vulgar a person as a Bull Connor or a Governor Wallace; on the other hand, a Wallace seems far more candid than a Yorty. Of course, there is an aesthetic difference between those who have bombed Negro churches in the "black belt" or those who have shot at civil rights workers and those whose dividend income is gained in fact, if not intentionally, from speculation in slum real estate or investment in enterprises which practice *de facto* discrimination in hiring, advertising, customer services, and the like. But the difference—at least in New Testament terms —is one of aesthetics, *not* ethics.

The massive indifference of the ordinary white citizen of good intentions is the moral equivalent of the perfidy of the white racists. The profound apathy of the white "moderates" is ethically tantamount to the radical impudence of the white racists.

That the difference between the pathological racists and the so-called moderates, in either North or South, is a matter of aesthetic distinction rather than ethical significance can be documented in all too many ways:

In the colleges and universities of the North, for all their venerable liberal traditions, there is almost universally only token integration. This has now been achieved even in most Southern colleges and universities. With a few exceptions—Dartmouth is one—there is no significant evidence of any inclination to move beyond tokenism in higher education in either section of the country or to address the issue which realistically remains the chief barrier to admission of qualified Negroes to college: the cost of tuition and room and board. Despite all the dropouts among Negro secondary-school students, there remain thousands of Negro students qualified for college who do not go—or even apply— because the costs of higher education are prohibitive.

Other factors affect the collegiate admission of Negro students, too. Many with college potential are diverted early in their public education into vocational and commercial courses. Many are reluctant to attend overwhelmingly white schools and become "exhibition" Negroes. Conventional recruitment and admissions procedures are often designed in a way which disadvantages the Negro applicant because, built into those interviewing and testing practices is the unarticulated assumption that the applicant will be a white middle-class type (much as a female applicant for law school is at a disadvantage because admissions formalities are still geared to male applicants).

Yet in the face of the most urgent need for increased access to higher educational training for Negroes, one repeatedly encounters the pathetically unrealistic rationalization of professing white "liberals" that Negro students already qualified for college entrance should be spared "special preference" in admissions lest they suffer "reverse discrimination" when, in fact, the effective barrier to their admission is simply lack of money.

There is also the gruesomely hypocritical matter of church investments, where mission boards, denominational institutions, local congregations and parishes, synodical and other regional authorities—not to mention legions of individual churchgoers—have the audacity to utter praises to the name of Christ while —again with a bare sprinkling of exceptions—profiting financially from a racism as evidenced by their endowment investments and by their current contracting, hiring, and spending policies. As to that, there is no important difference between the actual social witness on the side of racial segregation and discrimination among the churches and their related agencies in any part of the country.

Or, again, the moral kinship between the "moderate" and the professed racist can be seen by comparing the political regimes which both support and the similarity in tactics with respect to the racial crisis practiced by those administrations, both in the northern cities and in the southern hinterlands.

Just consider those tactics, as they have unfolded in the racial strife in both parts of the country:

Separation   In both North and South, regimes depend upon the separation of society between the ghetto and the rest of the society in order both to nurture a mentality of acquiesence and a capacity to endure hardship among the ghetto residents, on one hand, and to supply the ignorance and prejudicial stereotypes of other citizens about the ghetto people, on the other.

Concealment   In both, there must be substantial concealment of the suffering and deprivation of Negro citizens by keeping the actual conditions of ghetto existence out of the convenient sight of white citizens, a necessity often met by the routing of traffic under, over, around, but never through the blighted section.

Toleration   Demonstrations for equal rights, while undesirable, must often be tolerated within the ghetto where, sometimes, they tend to relieve tension but seldom impress the people outside; marches, however, outside the ghettos must, if possible, be stamped out.

Suppression   If violence does occur it must, at all costs, be localized within the ghetto and be suppressed by overwhelming force in the name, of course, of preserving law, order, and domestic tranquillity.

Rationalization When trouble does occur, the authorities must be quick to locate a scapegoat: in Harlem, hoodlums or drug addicts are always handy; in Alabama, blame the Communists and outside agitators. They must be sure, in applying this principle, to repeat the scapegoat charges *after* the trouble subsides in order to impress the people outside and, just as important, in order to provide them with an excuse for any future violence.

Procrastination Appease everybody by promising anything. Usually the ghetto people will be quiet for a while if a delegation is received at the executive mansion, allowed to refer to grievances (which, in such a reception, will be understated, generalized, and vague), and solicited with a few indefinite assurances that whatever should be done will be done. Sometimes inviting the delegation to pose for news photographs ameliorates tension and abets evasion. In case of emergency, however, keep promising to get to the bottom of things and to cure any legitimate ills or evils. If pressed further, though it is unlikely, appoint a committee (if truly desperate, try to keep one's head and name a commission, because it sounds more important and impartial) of prominent citizens to investigate. An investigation has an automatic, virtually magical effect, since people still suppose that investigation is a synonym for decisive action.

Distraction This maneuver is to be employed especially by mayors or governors in times of crisis. Attention can be pre-empted, for example, by staging a parade for astronauts, or by denouncing air pollution, or engaging in harmless controversy with a politician in the other party.

Tactics such as these—all too common in both North and South—cater to white apathy and thereby show contempt for the self-interest of those who are white and prosperous as much as for the rights of those who are black and poor.

Is Apathy Despair?

Perhaps only a psychiatrist could fathom the meaning of white apathy in the racial crisis. To me, however, the most significant single factor in the present situation, as ghetto violence embodies the profound despair of Negro people, is that the apathy of the great majority of white citizens may itself be a parallel form of despair.

Realism, enlightened self-interest, human reason—all argue convincingly for the constructive involvement of white citizens in working the social changes required to banish poverty, abolish the ghettos, and rehabilitate the nation economically, socially, and politically as one society. But apathy prevails. The reason cannot be any lack of public information or absence of warning about the crisis. It has been almost literally impossible, during the past decade, to read a newspaper or watch a newscast without gaining some awareness of the scope and ominous potentialities of the racial struggle. No white citizen, including those who still live in communities where there are no Negro residents, can plead ignorance to excuse noninvolvement. Perhaps white citizens have received some sort of mass inoculation. Perhaps, in fact, they have become so conscious of what is decadent in this society, so sensitive to the magnitude of the racial crisis, so aware of how many assumptions of white society are threatened, so astute about the upheaval in their own existence that would be wrought by significant integration of American public life that they have become paralyzed. So they read the news of demonstrations, and see photographs of riots, and hear the cries of the poor, but can no longer understand any of these things, allowing themselves to become victims of the repeated lies of the racists, or despairing of finding anything they can do which would not risk their property, their status, or their very lives. If they do not themselves become racists, they remain mute, pretend that the problem is somewhere else, fasten onto ingenious rationalizations, remind themselves that they are personally innocent of any offense toward black men, or revert to the banalities of brotherhood observances.

No one escapes this debilitating fatigue in some form or other.

I know that I am sick and tired of the racial crisis.

God knows how Negroes must feel, but I, as a white man, am now almost overwhelmed with the feeling that I do not want to hear anything more about it, or see anything more of it, or do anything more in it. I wish it could somehow be escaped or evaded or avoided.

There was another great crisis that this nation endured, within my own recollection, and about which I felt somewhat the same. During the Korean War, I was in the military service, though mercifully I was not stationed in Korea or called into combat, but, nevertheless, I vividly remember—as many others also must—an acute fatigue in which I did not want to hear or see or do anything more about that awful war. I wanted it to somehow evaporate and make no more demands on *me*. I am pretty sure that this sentiment, which was fairly prevalent, did not alleviate or abbreviate that war in any way; on the contrary, if anything, it must have contributed to its aggravation and prolongation.

Something similar is true now in the American racial crisis. *I* wish it would end without my being any longer or any more deeply involved. I would rather escape from what now happens to this nation. Yet I am certain both in my mind and in my guts that this exhaustion will not hasten the resolution—much less reconciliation—of the racial crisis: it can only frustrate and compound it.

A Matter of Survival

Everyone in the United States is now involved in the racial crisis. If there ever was an option on this subject, it has expired. The only issue that remains is *how* one is involved: obstinately, stupidly, irrationally—or with concern, intelligence, and compassion. On *that* matter, let us at last face some simple truths:

1) The racial crisis is not a "good cause" in the sense of some conventional charity like cancer research or aid for victims of disaster. Let whites renounce the romanticism of good works and the preposterous condescension of so-called liberalism: no white man is doing a favor for any Negro citizen by now advocating the ordinary rights of citizenship for the American Negro in 1966. If such involvement constitutes a favor, it is as much for the self-interest of whites as for any Negro citizen.

2) The Negro revolution must be considered within the context of the ethics and traditions of American social revolution. There is no great novelty to social revolution in America, and if the present crisis is seen as part

of this history, an astonishing fact emerges: all earlier revolts were characterized by the ethics and tactics of violence until the Negro revolution, with the possible exception of the woman suffrage movement (the women were apparently nonviolent in their demonstrations in the streets). Considering the vast numbers of citizens involved in the present revolution and the depth of their provocation, it is *incredible* that—so far—the Negro revolution has been for so long dominated by the ethics and tactics of nonviolence.

3) The dimensions of the Negro revolution are such that the very survival of the nation is at issue; the life and livelihood of every citizen is at stake. However damaging it may be morally and psychologically, the United States can probably survive, even while continuing to exclude the American Indian from the mainstream of its political and economic life. Politically and economically, the exile from American society of the Indian is hardly noticed, but the denial to twenty-two million Negro citizens of decent housing, educational opportunity, gainful employment, political responsibility, and free access to public accommodations is bound to threaten the survival of the nation for *everybody*. The exclusion of *that* many citizens from society jeopardizes the political freedom, economic solvency, psychological stability, and moral integrity of those who are *not* excluded just as much as those who are. White people must finally wake up to the fact that their own welfare is quite as much at issue as that of the Negro. At least let profound self-interest in the nation's survival finally end the paternalism of white men for black men in these United States.

4) Civil disobedience is not uncommon among Ameri-

cans. There are probably very few citizens who have not in one way or another indulged in acts of civil disobedience—especially in realms of the law concerning taxes, traffic, liquor sales and consumption, gambling, and sex. The laws of some jurisdictions invite disobedience by evasion—as in the case of New York State's divorce laws. All citizens need to remember, as we observe day-to-day developments in the racial crisis, how widespread civil disobedience really is.

Of course, there are different forms of civil disobedience. Until the riots the civil disobedience characteristic of the Negro revolution for the most part has been such that those who have disobeyed state and local laws—against which they were protesting—have willingly borne the consequences of their disobedience: they have submitted to arrest, endured prosecution, served jail sentences, and paid fines; even in their disobedience, they have upheld the rule of law.

The other form of civil disobedience opposes and denounces the rule of law as such, and is not only a disobedience to existing law but an attempt to overthrow the rule of law by taking the law into one's own hands. This is the civil disobedience of the lynch mob, the assassin, the Birmingham bomber. This is the civil disobedience that so far has been mainly practiced in the racial crisis by whites—especially in the South, but not only there—and to which all too often the police authorities themselves have been privy.

5) The Negro revolution is the eye of the hurricane, but it is not the whole storm. It is the most intense focus of contemporary social crisis, but that crisis involves many other citizens: all those who are poor, all those who are sick and uncared for, all those who are old and un-

wanted, all those who are young and neglected, all those whose skill and labor are made obsolete by automation—all those, in other words, who have either been cast off or outcast in America—all those for whom the promises of freedom and humanity and society remain unredeemed in America in the twentieth century.

That the crisis is acutely dramatized in the situation of the Negro citizen does not mean that if there were no Negroes in America, or if the Negroes continued to acquiesce in their own humiliation and oppression, this nation would escape the reformation that history now forces upon it. The truth is, rather, that American Negroes have become the authentic pioneers of a reconstruction of American society, sorely, even pathetically, needed by all Americans and of which we will all be beneficiaries should it come to pass.

A Dilemma in Ethics and Tactics

But will it come to pass? That is ominously doubtful.

It is now about twelve years since the Negro revolution broke into the headlines and has evidenced organization and direction. There have been all these years of peaceful protest: sit-ins and Freedom Rides and picketing and prayer vigils and marches. In that time, thousands of citizens have been arrested, thousands have lost their jobs, thousands have suffered shame and humiliation in the churches, in schools, in the courts, in hotels and parks and other public places, even in their own homes, in the pursuit of their rights as citizens.

The question which now plagues the civil rights movement is whether the ethics and tactics of nonviolence have

been vindicated in results. It is a very American, a very pragmatic question which now overtakes the Negro revolution. What does the American Negro citizen have to show for these long years of unparalleled dignity and humanity and restraint?

In the South, they have to show the decomposed remains of those sixty-one human beings, some Negroes, some whites, who sought to help citizens there to register to vote or who joined in peaceful demonstrations and protests, and who were murdered for it, and whose murderers have gone free. Hundreds of citizens can show you the scars on their bodies where they have been branded by cattle prods or bruised by police clubs or bitten by dogs. In one six-month period, in one southern jurisdiction alone, more than forty churches and homes were bombed and burned, and, like the homicides, this terrorism remains unpunished. If that furnishes a macabre consolation to any northern citizens, it need not—not any more—after one counts the homicides committed by the police during the northern ghetto riots and the multiple indignities which ghetto citizens endure in the North every day.

In both parts of the country, it is true, there is now token integration in some schools and in most colleges and universities, but tokenism is all it is almost anywhere. Meanwhile, the churches remain steadfastly segregated, with but rare exceptions, and the unions have been far slower to desegregate than many businesses.

The Congressional legislation of 1964 and 1965—the Civil Rights Act and the Voting Rights Bill—have been the two most tangible results of the pressures of peaceful protest: the former was at least responsive to the March on Washington, the latter to the Selma-Montgomery March. Yet the impact of both of these measures, as necessary as each was and as significant as both are, has been chiefly localized in the South. There, even before the public accommodations section, in many cities white businessmen had acknowledged the breakdown of segregation as an economic institution and had voluntarily opened their shops and restaurants and hotels to Negroes, though comparatively few southern Negroes can afford to patronize them regularly. In the northern jurisdictions, local legislation had long since pretty much covered the scope of the new federal laws, and the patterns of *de facto* segregation had long since been established; thus the new federal acts have had little practical impact.

When, therefore, the pragmatic question is asked—Have the tactics of nonviolence yielded significant results?—the truthful answer must be: much more so in the South than in the North, but only at an enormous cost in death and human suffering. And nonviolence has not produced, generally, changes in the practical, day-to-day lives and livelihoods of the ordinary Negro citizens of the land, while only *that* sort of change can possibly vindicate the nonviolent leadership in the civil rights movement.

Thus the Negro revolution has been plunged into a profound tactical crisis. Marches and sit-ins have never been as effective tactically in the North as they have been in the South, and when other forms of peaceful protest—like the school boycotts advocating the busing of students to achieve integration and quality education—have been attempted in the North, they have met with massive opposition from the incumbent political authorities and school boards, as well as from white parents and teachers. White intransigence has frustrated most forms of peaceful protest in the North and has, in fact, served to discredit nonviolence as a viable means of social protest.

Meanwhile, as the Vietnam war has expanded and the demonstrations against that war have become more numerous and frequent, many civil rights advocates committed to nonviolence are bewildered as to what can be done tactically, because they see that the antiwar movement has elicited such a wide public hostility to peaceful demonstrations about anything. In this same period, too, the despair of ghetto residents has erupted in violence. These pressures make it most difficult to maintain a nonviolence strategy in the tactics and ethics of the Negro revolution.

The kind of social change which has impact upon the practical lives of the multitudes of Negro citizens has not been launched by these years of peaceful protest, nor is there much evidence it has even entered the minds of most white citizens. Thus, the spirit of revenge is loose to prey upon the frustration and despair which American Negroes have inherited from three centuries of slavery and segregation. The mood becomes more militant and aggressive and explosive as each moment passes. There is the passionate conviction that it is better not to live than to be a Negro in the United States—North or South—so what is to be lost by turning to violent assault upon white society and white property and white people?

A Catharsis in Conscience?

Some remain optimistic that the Negro revolution reached a decisive climax in the voting rights demonstrations in the black belt of the Deep South. The long-suffering patience of Negro citizens was about to be recompensed; the conscience of white citizens, notably of the middle class, was finally aroused. After all, the ruthlessness of the rout of the Selma marchers on that awful Sunday in March, 1965, by the posse and the troopers provoked a flood of new entrants into the civil rights struggle who had never been involved in direct action before. Among them were some very important personages in the nation—leaders of the white establishment in the North and the West, ranking members of the ecclesiastical hierarchy of practically all the churches, heirs of some of the first families in the land, along with nuns and ordinary clergy and students who were also novices in the racial crisis. The President became more emphatic in his advocacy of equal suffrage and justice for Negro citizens than any president has ever been, and the Congress rallied to his side in a way without precedent in matters of civil rights legislation. Negro citizens of Alabama actually gathered at the state capital, surrounded by a great host of witnesses, to petition for the redress of their grievances. Multitudes of other Americans, if not moved to direct involvement, at least were at last shocked into sympathy, and many even walked a mile or two to their local courthouses or congregated in churches to evidence that. Nothing, it has been now much repeated, would be the same again: the great turning point had happened.

Not everyone regards these events as so climactic. Some had, at the time, the temerity to cite, for example, the difference in the response of white citizens and public officials to the murders of Medgar Evers or Jimmie Lee Jackson as compared to the murders of James Reeb and Viola Liuzzo. I do not question the commitment or courage of the white victims; the only issue is the reaction of white society to the assassination of Negroes, on the one hand, and the assassination of whites, on the other. It appears that the difference *is* significant, not only in the zeal and alacrity with which the President himself responded but also in the outcry and indignation of white society. If such a view, which is held by some Negroes, seems unduly embittered, white people might profitably recall the uncounted numbers of Negro citizens who have been killed, tortured, maimed, and brutalized by the violence of white racists—sometimes including police, sometimes just ignored by the police—during these years of protest and agony. This is a legacy of the racial crisis which can neither be disowned by white men nor readily forgiven by black.

Was Selma the symbol of the turning point in the revolution? It seems both premature and perilous to say so. The nation is now entering on the momentous and traumatic task of reconstructing society so that a citizen may not only vote but work and have the education requisite for both, live in a decent home in any neighborhood, obtain a mortgage or a loan to start a business, travel where he pleases, hold any public office he can win in a fair and free election, even, if he would like to do so, be a member of any congregation in the Church. For that struggle, all who enlisted at Selma are needed back in their home communities, along with literally millions more for whom Selma was only another newscast. I do not challenge the motives of any of the very important white people—much less the unimportant ones—who descended on Alabama, but the authenticity of white involvement in Selma depends upon the vigor and persistence of these same citizens, and many others like them, in every sector of American society where racism is still a fact. Until white commitment is verified in that way, and it has yet to be, Selma remains some feigned expiation—no climax but a mere catharsis.

Selma could have been a historic turning point if, on that

terrible Sunday when the posse charged the citizens, legions of contented, prosperous white people had finally realized the tragic course of events and had resolved to reverse their direction. But since Selma very little has happened to support the optimism created by the event. White apathy has not been exorcised nor has the despair of Negroes in the ghettos been absolved. On the contrary, as far as I can discern, there has been a hardening of white apathy and a fermenting of black despair. The nation is not apt to be spared holocaust.

And so comes a day of wrath.

A Day of Wrath

As the day of wrath dawns, let it come as no surprise, especially to white men, either senators or common citizens. After all, what is involved is not merely the frustration of these past many years of peaceful protest, nor just the insensibility of the public authorities, nor just the complacency and default of white citizens, but the inheritance of the past three centuries of slavery and segregation.

No Negro child is born in this land, who has a responsible parent—and in this most Negro parents are responsible—who is not taken aside, at a tender age—at four or five, or when the child first goes to school—and told by his parents what it means to be a Negro in America and hears recited the whole saga of the Negro's exile from American society. Thereafter, for *that* child, it is not just his own experience and endurance of discrimination or rejection which are *his* cause, but now he is an heir to the suffering and travail of his whole people, just as each

Jewish child who is born becomes an heir to the exile of
the Jews from biblical times right up to the present, including in Nazi Germany, the Soviet Union, and, alas,
many parts of the United States.

Yet, as the Bible testifies, the exile of the Jews is as
much an inheritance of the Egyptians and, now, the
Germans. Both captive and captor have the *same* inheritance. And the exile of the American Negro is also
the inheritance of white men in America. But white
parents have not been wise enough to tell their children
so. Why should it be surprising, then, that white men—
confronted with the present crisis—respond ineptly, fearfully, stupidly, hysterically?

As the day of wrath comes, let it be at least seen that
captors are always prisoners just as much as captives are,
and that the emancipation of those in bondage is the only
way to set free those who have kept them in bondage.

As the day of wrath begins, it should finally become
clear that the real recalcitrant in the American racial
crisis is not the so-called die-hard segregationist or the
pathological racist but respectable, sane, sincere, benevo-
lent, earnest people, church members and devout liberals.
They do not hate Negroes, but they also do not know
that paternalism and condescension are as much forms
of alienation as enmity and hate. They are the white people
who, right now, are asking the question, "What does the
Negro want?" failing to understand that this very question
assumes that it is *their* prerogative to dispense to the
Negro what the Negro will get. In that very assumption is
the essence of white supremacy. And it is *that* mentality—
which most white Americans share—that must be exorcised if there is to be reconciliation between black men
and white men in America.

On the day of wrath, however, as things stand now, the prospect is *not* reconciliation—the prospect is that Negro violence will be met by overwhelming counterviolence by the police—probably the Army—which the white Establishment of America has at its command. If that day comes, the frightful peril for all Americans is that this nation will take an irrevocable step into a police state, and the possibility of freedom for all citizens will be aborted.

In the day of wrath, what could save the nation from such a calamity is the recognition by white people that every hostility or assault by Negroes against whites and against white society originates in the long terrible decades of exclusion and rejection of Negroes by white men. Negro violence now is the offspring of white supremacy. The sins of the fathers are indeed visited upon their sons.

A Hope for Absolution

Now as it comes to pass that nonviolence is increasingly forsaken in the Negro Revolution, there is, I believe, a most specific witness to which white Christians in America are summoned and which I gladly commend to them. The witness of the white Christian, on such a day, must surely be the same as the witness already given by so many Negro Christians during those long years of anguish and protest: the witness of the Cross.

The Cross is not a mere religious symbol; it is profaned when it becomes that in the minds of men. Nor is the Cross just some reference to an event which took place once upon a time but which has no reality in the present day. The Cross means not only the consignment of Christ to death but His triumph over the power of death on behalf of the world. The Cross means the invincible power of God's love for the world, even though all the world betrays, denies, abhors, fears, or opposes the gift of His love for the world. The Cross means voluntary love which is undaunted by any hostility or hatred or violence or assault. The Cross means voluntary love which is not threatened by death. The Cross means voluntary love which perseveres no matter what. The Cross means the gift of love even to one's own enemy—even to the one who would take one's life.

Whenever it comes to pass that white men *who are Christians* are attacked by Negroes and endure ridicule or humiliation or interference or taunting torture; whenever it comes to pass that white Christians are exposed to the loss of their possessions, or status, or jobs, or property, or homes, or even families; if one's own life itself is at issue, let the witness of the white Christian—for himself, for all white men, and, in fact, for all men everywhere—be the witness of the Cross.

Even if the knife is at the belly, let the white Christian not protest. Let him receive the assault recklessly, without precaution, without resistance, without rationalization, without extenuation, without a murmur.

Is this asking for too much from white American Christians? Have they too long forgotten and forsaken the Cross?

God has neither forgotten nor forsaken the Cross.

This is why there is *no other way* that this enormous, desperate, growing accumulation of guilt, shame, estrangement, and terror can be absolved. There has never been— for any man, anywhere, at any time—any other way. In the work of God in our midst, reconciling black men and white men, there is no escape from the Cross.

Chapter Four

The Orthodoxy of Radical Involvement

His purpose in dying for all was that men, while still in life, should cease to live for themselves, and should live for him who for their sake died and was raised to life. With us therefore worldly standards have ceased to count in our estimate of any man; even if once they counted in our understanding of Christ, they do so now no longer. When anyone is united to Christ, there is a new world; the old order has gone, and a new order has already begun.

II Corinthians 5:15–17

MULTITUDES of earnest and well-intentioned church members who want to remain loyal to the Church are greatly agitated nowadays about what they regard as an unwarranted intrusion and involvement of the Church and of some of their fellow churchmen in controversial public issues. They are worried when they see the Church "taking sides" in our political crises, in direct action in the racial struggle which engulfs this society, in attention —however cursory it still is—given to the persistence of poverty amid fantastic affluence, or in protests against the American foreign military policy (particularly in Vietnam), to name only the few most desperate and troublesome contemporary public issues.

Many local members of all Christian denominations are afraid that the Church will be compromised by involvement in worldly affairs. Their concern is that the Church of Christ and the Christian people remain outside of, or above, or withdrawn from the political and social conflicts which separate men in their secular lives.

Let the Church, they say, remain pure and undefiled.

Let the Church, at least, be one place left where men can contemplate their God, devote themselves to "spiritual" things, and get away from conflict and dissension.

Let the Church be a shrine of peace of mind and positive thinking, of the blessed assurance of better things somewhere, sometime, someplace beyond this realm. Let the Church be uncontaminated by worldly business. Let the Church be a place of rest and abstinence from worldly cares. Let the Church be a refuge from the world. Let the Church be a sanctuary for escape.

This is a common and popular view within the Church in this society. It is likely the dominant point of view among laity—especially in the churches of American Protestantism. It is not, however, the point of view of the

New Testament Church. Hear, for example, the Letter
of James:

> Religion that is pure and undefiled before God and
> the Father is this: to visit orphans and widows in their
> affliction, and to keep oneself unstained in the world.
>
> James 1:27

There are many echoes of the same theme throughout
the New Testament, not only in the historic ministry of
Christ himself in his own association with publicans and
sinners: prostitutes, politicians, tax collectors, the dis-
eased, demoniacs, the poor, soldiers, thieves, hoodlums
and, even, ecclesiastical authorities, but also in the later
Apostolic ministry of the Church of Christ with its
emphatic stress upon the posture of the Church as in,
though not of, the world.

It is not possible to listen to any letters of the New Testament without hearing this same theme. And the same can
be said, I do believe, of that most neglected work of all
in the Bible—the Book of Revelation to John.

But, for now, take the passage from James. James is a
book of practical theology, as it is now called in the
seminaries (thereby obscuring the fact that all theology
which has integrity in the Gospel is inherently practical).
James counsels that the practice of the Christian faith
means an involvement in the world which does not con-
form the Christian to the world. Visit orphans, comfort
widows, care for the unwanted, seek out the outcasts, love
your enemy but *in a way* which leaves one free from the
world; free from all worldly conformities; free from the
secular ethics of success; free from the idols of security,
riches, fame, property, popularity; free from the claims of

ideology and class and race; free from self-indulgence—
and, what is finally the same thing, attempts at self-justification; free from the wiles of the Devil, that is, free, at
last, from the power of death militant in this world.

Be in but not of the world. Be involved but be unstained. How can such an apparent paradox be resolved?
What sort of involvement in the world is authorized in an
orthodox comprehension and practice of the Christian
faith? What does engaging in social and political conflict
have to do with the understanding, in Christian orthodoxy,
of Jesus Christ, or with the nature of the Church as such,
or with the esoteric existence of the Church in public
worship in the liturgy, or, for that matter, with the meaning of being a baptized person? What are the marks of
Christian involvement in this world?

Pietists, Pharisees, and Do-gooders

Considering both the sectarianism and secularization
of the churches in the United States, one must first make
clear what is meant by orthodoxy. Those churchly folk
who regard the world as evil condemn involvement in
social crises and public controversy in the name of the
purity of their faith. That is a kind of orthodoxy. The
Selma vestrymen who turned away churchmen who had
been demonstrating for voting rights complained that the
presence in worship of these clergy and laymen would
profane the religion of their parish (which, no doubt, was
literally true). The vestry was defending a certain orthodoxy. The self-assured activists who suppose themselves to
be ushers of the Kingdom of God also claim orthodoxy.

The question becomes: which orthodoxy? that of the

pietists? that of the pharisees? or that of the do-gooders?

It was to defend orthodoxies such as these that Jesus Christ was tried, condemned, and delivered to death. But in the deliverance of Jesus Christ from the power of death the precedent of genuine Christian orthodoxy was established in this world. The precedent of Christian orthodoxy is Christ Himself, His own ministry in this world and the veracity of His Resurrection; it is both the consummation of the whole biblical testimony and the genius of the witness of the Apostolic Church.

So it was and is and will be. The precedent of Christian orthodoxy is unchanging, though all else change. Christ is the same yesterday and today and tomorrow. If, in the churches nowadays, the Bible is sometimes read but seldom heard, the Word of God is not muted because the people are deaf. If the historic creeds are recited but not confessed, the precedent is not repealed by such apostasy. If the Gospel is dramatized liturgically, but churchgoers treat this action as simply an empty ritual, the good news is not vitiated because men are superstitious.

Some will complain that the days are too urgent to afford inquiry into the authority in Christian orthodoxy for action in society. When the nation is engulfed in a crisis more momentous than the Civil War, they think there is no time to spend on what they regard as doctrinal niceties. After all, preoccupation with the theological rationalization of action has too often hindered the churches from any active commitment except to their own institutional survival. Did not the fastidiousness of German Christians about theology nourish their apathy toward Nazism?

I have considerable sympathy for such impatience. So much needs to be done if the nation is merely to survive the racial crisis that one must be grateful for those few people who are seriously working for the integration of American society, whether they call themselves Christians or not and however mixed their motivations. Nevertheless, the complaints of the impatient are based on a misconception of orthodoxy, as if it were a pedantic reduction of the Gospel to a propositional scheme which could furnish a basis for application and involvement.

Christian orthodoxy, however, is both historic and existential. It is not to be confused with doctrinal formulations—though these have a certain use and, in a given instance, may be literally true. The substance of Christian orthodoxy, in other words, is no less and none other than the very event of Christ.

Christology and Ethics

Let us put aside all secular legends of Christ and, instructed by II Corinthians, no longer count worldly standards important in our understanding of Christ. Let us renounce the well-behaved Jesus innocent of scandal and controversy; the Jesus of superstition memorialized in dashboard statuettes and lucky charms; the fanciful, ineffectual, effeminate, effete Jesus of the cinema whom the multitudes found irresistibly attractive; the soft, spiritual, sentimental Jesus of Sallman and other vulgar caricatures; the farsighted Jesus teaching democracy to primitive people centuries before the French and American Revolutions; the imaginary Jesus thought to be an unfortunate victim of a gross violation of due process of law.

Let us, at the same time, forget all religious ideas of Christ; although propagated within the churches, they are only slightly disguised secular notions of Him. Let us, in the name of Christian orthodoxy, expose and repudiate the fairy-tale Jesus of Sunday-school story books; the ridiculous Jesus fashioned after the manner of the white Anglo-Saxon Protestant; the unapproachable Jesus captive in tabernacles; the shiny, fragrant Jesus of snow-white raiment unspoiled by sweat or blood or the smell of fish; the religiose Jesus, an ascetic too esoteric for this world.

Let us also leave behind, as St. Paul counsels, the elementary disputes of tradition about the "divinity" of Christ versus the "humanity" of Jesus. This is not so much because they often hide error as because they usually sow confusion; they are not entirely irrelevant, but they encourage dissipation, diverting attention from the actual event of Jesus Christ in this world and thus hindering the actual event of the Christian witness in this world.

Instead, let us behold Jesus Christ as the one whom God has shown Christ to be in this world: the new Adam— the true man—the man reconciled in God.

Reconciled *in* God: the preposition helps to emphasize the scope and grandeur of the reconciliation wrought by God in Himself. In the reconciliation in Christ, God and man live as one; encompassed in Him is at once the integrity and wholeness of both God and man, and the unity and love between them and every person and all things. The outreach of the reconciliation which is God's work extends to the whole of creation throughout all places and times. Jesus Christ is the embodiment of that reconciliation. Reconciliation, in terms of Christian orthodoxy, is not some occasional, unilateral, private happening, but, much more than that, the transcendent, universal, and profoundly political event in all time.

Reconciliation is a political event. I realize that, for

some, politics is a loathsome word, but, after all, it refers only to the body of interrelationships of men and institutions in this world. Reconciliation is the event, as II Corinthians testifies, of a new order of corporate life of men and institutions inaugurated in the world in Christ. In view of this order, it is impossible to consider the reconciliation of one man outside of, or separately from, the estate of all other men and institutions, that is, *politically*. No man speaks truthfully of being reconciled to God who has not suffered reconciliation in God, who is not, in other words, now reconciled with himself, with all other men, and with all things in the whole of creation.

The event of Jesus Christ, the reconciliation of the whole of creation in time and in the fullness of time, is in behalf of all men; all men benefit from it whether or not they realize it, or desire it, or even like it. It is, simply, the gift of God, acting, as it were, all by Himself among men and in the place of men in this world. It is not something which a man may in any way deserve, purchase, grasp, accomplish, or otherwise procure. As with any gift, it may be opposed, just as Mary resisted Christ's vocation; or it may be refused, just as the multitudes rejected Jesus' ministry; or it may be condemned, just as the ecclesiastical authorities sought to destroy Christ; or it may be dishonored, just as Judas betrayed the Lord; or it may be denied, just as the disciples remained so consistently incredulous until Pentecost, when they endured their own reconciliation with themselves and with the world in God.

All this remains true today. Despite the popularity of heresy within the churches, though men are enthusiastic in their unbelief, even if many men worship their own doubts, and in spite of the public affection for death, noth-

ing avails against the reconciliation of which Christ is the
pioneer, the advocate, and the surrogate.

As in earlier times, to be a Christian, a member of
Christ's Body, is to be established already, here and now,
in this world, in an estate of reconciliation which at once
accepts one's self and embraces the whole world. To be a
Christian is to receive and know and participate in the un-
conditional, extravagant, inexhaustible, expendable love
of God for all that He has made and called into being. To
be reconciled by the virtue of Christ is to be restored to
one's own identity in the Word of God, which authorized
one's life in the first place, and to be free to identify and
affirm the integrity of all other life in that same Word.

To be a Christian, to be already reconciled, means to
love the world, all the world, just as it is—*unconditionally*.

The Ethics of Reconciliation

Because reconciliation is not private and personal so
much as it is public and political, because reconciliation
is a new estate in which all relationships without exception
or excuse are transfigured, it is celebrated and manifested
as such: reconciliation is, simply, lived.

Such a witness is not always self-evident but often secret.
It is not likely that it will be welcome in the world or
rewarded in the churches. Paradoxically, it is an effort-
less witness in which a man ceases to live for himself and
lives now for Christ (which means, at the same time,
precisely, to live for the world), but it is not an easy
witness, since it is very difficult for men to despair of
trying to justify themselves. It requires so many risks of
death. After all, the most radical self-acceptance is needed

to actually love the world as it is. Yet, there it is: reconciliation in Christ means loving this world absolutely. The time is immediate, not later on; the place is here, not any other or after place. Reconciliation means acceptance, not approval; it is a matter of voluntary love, not religious obligation; it is marked by gladness and is without guile.

Concretely, in the present circumstances of racial estrangement in the United States, reconciliation means, among other things, that those Christians committed to direct action for equal rights for all citizens should nevertheless persevere in loving the humanity of the wide assortment of others assembled in political and social and religious opposition to integration in American public life. It means that worldly standards in the estimate of other men no longer count, since all such traditions and ways are transcended in reconciliation. Specifically, those Christians who marched in Selma were called to affirm the essential humanity of Sheriff Clark, even though they have been beaten on his order. It means loving the person of a Mayor Wagner or of a Mayor Daley or a Mayor Yorty while at the same time opposing the social apathy and moral indifference such politicians typify. It is, terribly and wonderfully, forgiving the Ku Klux Klan, though they have not yet abandoned their violence and treachery. It requires caring for the John Birchers as human beings, even in the face of their hysteria and contempt. It is loving others though they hate themselves. It means, finally, loving your neighbor in the realization that each man's real neighbor is the man who is his enemy. The commandment to love one's neighbor, and the example, in Christ, of love for one's enemy are ultimately synonymous.

This is a point, of course, at which Christians are often challenged by secular contemporaries, especially those with whom they happen to be associated in particular issues and causes in society. Such challenges are temptations to renounce reconciliation. To the secular mind the ethics of reconciliation is bound to seem reckless and rather stupid. Why give any comfort to one's enemy? How can a man love one who opposes his most serious convictions and, thereby, assaults his very existence? From what condition or threat are men saved in the reconciliation in Christ that a man should embrace his enemy without first defeating him, or procuring his surrender, or at least persuading the enemy that he is uninformed, benighted, or deliberately wicked? According to secular wisdom, love inherently requires approval, or significant agreement, or the humiliation of an opponent by condescending to let bygones be bygones after having beaten him. Love is, thus, conditional: to love one's enemy in the midst of conflict while the enemy is seeking your destruction is folly. Every worldly ethics assumes that the drama of history is some conflict between good and evil, and our effort should be to distinguish accurately between the two, and then earnestly pursue the good for its own sake while teaching other men to do the same.

The ethics of reconciliation, however, understands that the moral conflict of this world is far more ambiguous and radical than that. The basic confession of the Gospel of Christ acknowledges that men do not possess, either personally or socially, the knowledge of good and evil, and that ultimate moral knowledge is the unique prerogative of God, who judges all men and all things as He pleases.

At the same time, both personally and socially, men *do* inherit a transient moral knowledge which is wholly relative to themselves and to their own survival. Men, as well as nations, races, classes, and other institutions, can more or less discern what is good for them—that is, what will tend to defend, prolong, or prosper their own existence. But that which is regarded as good in this sense is never known in this world to be coincident with God's judgment of each decision and action and omission of every man and nation.

In terms of the ethics of the world, of such transient moral knowledge relative to their own mere survival which men and nations do inherit, in the present racial crisis it is transparent to human reason (though racism has corrupted the rationality of many citizens) that the American nation cannot survive as a democratic society without the deliberate and speedy integration of the country's public life. Whatever assessment may be made of the past, of the long era of slavery and this last century of segregation and discrimination (though I do not see how any very positive assessment can be made), the issue now posed is that the American idea of society cannot outlive racism in either its vulgar and violent or subtle and passive forms. Integration in America is good for America because it has become the moral requirement of the nation's survival.

However, the fact that integration is a prior condition for American survival does not make integration the moral equivalent of reconciliation. On the day, if it comes (a matter now pathetically in doubt), of genuine integration of American public life, though every other citizen may be content, Christians will not be satisfied. Rather, they will be saying: "This is not enough, for a new society has been inaugurated in this world in Christ and the Church of Christ, where it lives, is the embassy of that society and beckons all men into it. This is the society of reconciliation, and no society which men may have or seek in this world can approximate or displace it, and the Christian social conscience is not satisfied until all the world is one society in Christ."

Integration is good if this nation is to linger and last a little longer, but men, and all things, are reconciled in this world—that is, freed from imprisonment in death—only in the Body of Christ.

Eschatology and Ethics

The drama of history, exposed in the insight of the Gospel, is not a conflict between evil and good, as secular ethics supposes, but concerns the power of death in this world and how death is overpowered in this life by the power of the Resurrection. It is the juxtaposition of death and Resurrection that authorizes the Christian involvement in worldly affairs of all sorts and that verifies the eschatological hope which Christians have for all men and the whole of creation.

The present age is one of death, not evil; it is the era of death in the sense that all men and all things are vulnerable to death, but, more significantly, in the sense that *right now* in the midst of life, all men and all things are prisoners of death's power. Creation is fallen, to use the traditional language of Christian orthodoxy. The Fall does not mean that the world is evil, or that men and their institutions are bad, or that either men or principalities have an inclination toward wickedness. The Fall means, rather, that all of creation exists in bondage to death, without any power to prevail against death. In the Fall, death reigns over men and nations and ideas, and over all that is, as a living, militant, pervasive and, apparently, ultimate power—in other words, as *that* which gives moral significance to everyone and everything else. Death is the ruling idol which all other idols—race, nationalism, religion, money, sex, and all their counterparts—worship and serve, and to which men in their turn give honor and sacrifice through their idolatries.

It is proof of the success of death that men are deceived into supposing that death does not exist as the ruler of this world (indeed, sometimes death is so successful that men suppose that they are immortal and that death does not exist at all!), and it is part of the foolishness of men's arrogance to blame all that seems to them wrong in this world upon themselves (which is, of course, just a perverse way of claiming that men can set things right and save themselves). Yet plainly, death is aggressively at work all the time and everywhere and, more plainly, all that is wrong in this world cannot be attributed to the mere behavior of men.

It is odd that men are so deceived, considering just how manifest and obvious the presence of death is in the common life of the world. Illness and injury offer constant evidence, though a number of sects and so-called scientists flourish by denying them. Loneliness, too, is endured by each of us, an experience in which a man is in dread not that he be left alone but that he does not exist, since nothing that he knows, including himself, affirms his existence. To be unemployed—unneeded, unwanted, unused by society—instills in men the fear of death. Even those able to store up a fortune in savings and investments for the sake of their "security" are, ironically, motivated by the selfsame fear. When the social scientists complain that the rigors of urban existence or the impact of technological change upon persons is "dehumanizing," they are pointing to death at work, whether they know what they are talking about or not. War, famine, plague, to be consigned to poverty or in bondage to wealth, all forms of personal estrangement and all separations of society according to worldly standards of class or sex or race or nation or ideology or what not—all these are the signs of death busy in the world, evidence of its victory over men and the rest of creation.

Theologically, death is the reality of separation from God, but the economy of that phrase, so often invoked in the churches, should not hinder the understanding of its scope. To be separated from God is to be alienated from the ground and being of life itself, and, therefore, from all life. To be separated from God is to be cut off from one's own self and from other human beings and from all things as well. To be so profoundly estranged is to be dead in truth, just as when one is buried in the ground, or, meanwhile, to be as good as dead in that way now in the present age in which all relationships are marred and sundered and evidently bereft of any meaning more significant than the breach itself.

The power of death which reigns in the world has racial separation as one of its acolytes. Thus, the concern of the Christian in the contemporary racial crisis in America is radically different from that of those secularists who see that racism is a monstrous contradiction in a democracy and that segregation is so politically corrupt and economically costly that it imperils the survival of the nation. Hopefully, Christians will be informed enough to share those insights, but they do not represent a Christian conscience about racism. For the Christian, it is not just that racism is morally wrong for this society but, rather, that in any of its vulgar or sophisticated forms it is a sign of death at work. Racism is one of the ways in which men and institutions suffer that separation from one another which represents their own loss of identity in the Fall.

Let us recall Sheriff Clark, not now for his senseless brutalization of Negro citizens but for the disavowal of *his own humanity* which his actions have demonstrated. The terrible thing about a Sheriff Clark is the vehemence with which he rejects his own life by his persecution of the lives of others. In other words, racism—among other forms of alienation—is a hostility to other human life which constitutes a repudiation of one's own life, and is the essence of that separation from God which is the state of death. Despite the elementary controversies about literalism and myth—that is really what the Genesis saga of Adam is about—to be radically estranged from God means the incapacity to love another, which originates in rejection of one's own life. That is, as well, the truth embodied in the Dual Commandment—to be reconciled to God means to love one's own humanity in a way which affirms all of life.

But let Christians remember that integration is not the equivalent of reconciliation. Segregation is a synonym, theologically, for one of the works of death, but integration is not the same thing as freedom from death, even though it may be a process through which some will be emancipated from those apparitions of death which masquerade in racism.

And make no mistake about it. Unwilling as I am to furnish any pretexts for rationalization to anyone who refuses civil rights for all citizens, there are frightening indications of the meddling of death in the civil rights movement, just as it (the more precise pronoun, in Christian orthodoxy, is *he*) does in every other thing.

Death is tempting some to support integration as a convenience to their own justification, as a demonstration of moral rightness and self-righteousness, as a means of purchasing the ease and silence of their own consciences. Death, in other words, is occupied in the civil rights movement luring some to behold integration as an idol, and though it be a more benign idol, subjectively speaking, than segregation or slavery, the most that can be expected by advocates of civil rights—and the worst that can happen, the segregationists can be assured—is that public integration will salvage the nation from the moral suicide of racism. The world will thereby be edified about the American idea of society, but the world will not be saved by so puny a human accomplishment.

There is also the danger both for society and the churches that the involvement of some Christians in the racial crisis will result in revival of a simplistic social gospel similar to that which entrapped so many Christians during the social reconstruction in the aftermath of the Depression, in which it was so widely assumed that the issue was the mere existence of evil in its transient and relative sense rather than the real presence of death in this world—even in America.

Meanwhile, let neither the self-conscious nor the *de facto* white supremists—that is, most white citizens—have any unwarranted pride in the foibles and ambiguities of those within the civil rights movement. Let none of them suppose that death has been preoccupied in tempting integrationists only. They are only too willing to believe that acceptance of what is being forced upon them is an indication of their generosity. An evasion such as this is simply another temptation in the repertoire of death.

Death is now encouraging many clergy and laity from

the churches to regard the civil rights movement as a parachurch, as a secular movement which has more similarity, reality, and integrity as *Church* than the more familiar, conventional, and prosperous bureaucracy called Church in the American white Establishment. Unfortunately, those who have this view imitate in their supposed real Church the same thing against which they protest in the churches of bourgeoise society—a cheap and quick conformity to the world. Those who now regard the civil rights movement as a parachurch suffer from the same kind of delusion as those, for example, who equate laissez-faire capitalism with the Gospel, or who think of Gandhi as a "better Christian" than most professing Christians (whereas he was just a more mature human being than most professing Christians), or who think that God prefers any worldly standard over any other.

The actual Church, the Church of Christ, which lives in this history—not to be confused with any status quo in secular existence, including the contemporary denominations and sects which claim the name in their incorporations—exists as a society in this world where men already suffer their reconciliation, where men already discern each ingenious assault of death and are yet set free because God's grace is so extravagant and relevant. The Church, as such, lives wherever men recognize that the only real enemy is death and not something so trivial as their own evil, all the while remembering that their own malice is not thereby erased or discounted. The Church is wherever there are no longer any separations in any dimension of creation, whether within one's self, or with others, or with any things, or between and among any of them.

The Church of Christ is, quite literally, the Body of Christ, engaging in His witness in this world. Thus the

Church is given to the world and established in the world by God, not to offer some religious apologetic for any secular ideas or hopes, however appealing some of them may be. Instead, the Church lives now as the new society in the midst of the old, as the reconciled community when all else is broken and distorted, as the new creation during the era of the Fall, as the example and vindication of life transcending the power of death. The Church of Christ is the prophet and pioneer, actually the herald and foretaste of God's own accomplishment in Christ, confronting every assault and disguise of death, and exposing and overcoming them all within this history, in order to restore men to life here and now.

Hence the vocation of the Church of Christ in the world, in political conflict and social strife, is inherently eschatological. The Church is the embassy of the eschaton in the world. The Church is the image of what the world is in its essential being. The Church is the trustee of the society which the world, now subjected to the power of death, is to be on that last day when the world is fulfilled in all things in God.

To the world as it is, then, the Church of Christ is always, as it were, saying both Yes and No simultaneously. They are, in fact, the same word, for they each say that the end of the world is its maturing in Christ. It is that maturity of human life in society which the Church as the reconciled community foreshadows in this world.

Thus, also, the Church is constantly engaged, in and through her actual existence as the new society, in beseeching the end of the world; therefore, the Church is always authorized to complain, for the sake of this world, about everything in this world. By the mercy of God, the inherent, invariable, unavoidable, intentional, unrelenting

posture of the Church in the world is one of radical protest and profound dissent toward the prevailing status quo
of secular society, whatever that may be at any given time,
however much men boast that theirs is a great society.

Churchly Unity as Worldly Witness

The estate of the Church of Christ as the archetypal
society of mankind is, of course, what gives urgency and
significance for the world to the ecumenical movement
now taking place within all the churches of historic Christendom. This has been chiefly manifest in our time by the
emergence, first of all, of the World Council of Churches,
embracing most of Protestantism, Eastern Orthodoxy, and
Anglicanism, more lately by the Vatican Council in the
Roman Catholic Church, and most recently by overtures
of friendship and gestures of social concern among some
of the Evangelical sects and denominations.

The rationale and integrity of the ecumenical movement does not consist in the enhancement of the grandeur,
power, or influence of the Church of Christ as such. Nor
is it aimed at achieving ecclesiastical, ritualistic, or dogmatic conformity among the churches. The ecumenical
enterprise is not fundamentally a religious movement, but
is most significant in its secular aspects. The unity of the
Church of Christ *is* the essence of the public and political
witness of the Church in the world.

The unity of the Church of Christ is a gift of God
bestowed in the birth and constitution of the Church at
Pentecost.

The unity of the Church is a *gift,* not something sought

or grasped or attained, but, as with any gift, something which may be refused or dishonored or misused.

The gift of unity is, in the first instance, something which belongs to God. He gives at Pentecost something of His own, something of Himself, to the Church. This same unity given to the Church at Pentecost is vouchsafed for all men baptized into the body of the Church since Pentecost.

The unity which God gives the Church is not given for the sake of the Church, to be merely prized or praised therein, but to be the form and shape of the Church's love for, and service to, the world.

Nor does God give unity to the Church for His own sake, as if He needed anything at all, even the unity of those who call upon His name. It is for the sake of the world, for the sake of all persons and powers who do not or will not call upon God's name that unity is given to the Church, for it is in the unity of the Church that the world, in its profound disunity, may behold the unity into which God invites all men.

The unity of the Church of Christ, which is a gift of God, is the same unity revealed in the world in Christ Himself: that is, man reconciled to God and, within that unity, reconciled within himself, with all men, and with all creation. This is the unity which the Church receives as the representative of the world before God. It is the unity which the Church enjoys as the witness of God's reconciling work in the world. The unity given to the Church is the exemplification and forerunner of the restoration of unity for the whole of creation in Christ. *Hence the very unity of the Church is its authentic witness.*

Where the Church denies or rejects or perverts the gift of unity, the witness of the Church to the world is lost.

That is a loss which the Church suffers much more acutely than the world, though it must be remembered that God thereby suffers no loss at all. The disunity of the Church does not estop God's love for the world; it does, however, deprive the Church of the joy of witnessing to God's care for, and work in, the world.

Since God's love for the world is not dependent upon the unity of the Church, and His action in the world is not mitigated when the Church is not His witness, the world is not pardoned for its failure to acknowledge and honor God simply because of the Church's failure. The world is not excused from its unbelief by the collapse of the Church's witness in unity, but is thereby abandoned to death by the very people born of the Resurrection from death.

Disunity does not compromise or interrupt the Word of God for the world, but it does distort and even destroy the Church's witness to the Word of God in the world. The recovery of visible unity, which the world can see, comprehend, and recognize, does not mainly involve questions of ecclesiological uniformity, liturgical conformity, dogmatic nicety, regularity of discipline, or homogeneity of polity. What is to be established is the Church as a living people, a holy nation, manifest and militant in this world, embracing every diversity of mankind, here and now transcending all that separates, alienates, and segregates men from themselves, each other, or the rest of creation. The witness of the Church in and to a broken, divided, and fallen world is that of a new society in which worldly standards have ceased to count.

Is American society still torn by racial hostility? Where the Church of Christ lives in America it is not the model of integrated society, but much, much more than that: it is the community in which all races enjoy each other's company in reconciliation. Is the chasm between the rich and the poor deepening in the United States as technological change accelerates? Where Christ's Church is, all are poor because they are so rich in their love for one another and in their service to the world. Does the world account for the worth of men in age or inheritance or education or health or profession? In the Church which belongs to Christ the only status a man has is that which is bestowed upon him at birth and restored to him in Baptism; that is the bond of the new community, against which all status distinctions have lost meaning.

I am not talking about what the relation of the Church to the world *should be*. Not at all. I am confessing that this is what the Church of Christ *is*. Many will complain that the Church in this sense is difficult to locate or identify, but that does not alter its nature. The conformities of the churches in their divisions cannot be hidden. Nevertheless, the witness of the Church to the world is the image of what the whole of creation is and will be in the final reconciliation, and such a witness requires a unity in the Church which the world can directly and plainly behold. Any specific schemes or proposals for mergers or consolidation among the sects and denominations, any plans or prospects for reunion of the Church, must grasp and serve this end: Unity is integral to witness; the Church exists, not for God's sake or its own sake but merely for the sake of the world.

The unity of the Church, which is the witness of the Church, is not necessarily an institutional unification of the several churches, since such a witness requires a unity encompassing *all* diversities of human life. But this unity does require a total community of all who are baptized and profess the same biblical and apostolic faith, living in communion with one another now, and with the whole of the people of God who have gone before and who are yet to be, and sharing a versatile, manifold, but common and profoundly singular ministry for the world.

To put it most bluntly, the unity which is witness involves an organic union of all the churches in a shared common life in all things. This is quite different from having friendly relations and fraternal collaboration among the several churches of Protestantism, Orthodoxy, Anglicanism, and Rome, as welcome as that may be. Ultimately, it means the organic unity of all the churches for the sake of the world.

It is also what unity means in the beginning of the Church. The unity of the Church which is witness to the world is a gift of God in Pentecost. As the account relates (Acts 2), in Pentecost God is filling the Apostles with His Holy Spirit in a way which shows onlookers and strangers the universality of the Word of God, which discloses that the Word of God is addressed to all men everywhere and at all times, that it is present and active in this world and accessible to every man, whoever he may be. In Pentecost, the gift of the Spirit, which is one and the same for all who receive it, is given to the Church in a way which is versatile enough to reach and embrace all men in all of their diversities and divisions and separations.

Though the gift of the Spirit is manifold, it is not divisive of the Church. Though there are varieties of service within the ministry and witness of the Church, each is a manifestation of the same Spirit, each attests to the same Word of God. This Apostolic precedent of unity is both a unity

entrusted to the Church for the healing of worldly divisions
and a unity within the Church encompassing the full
variety of service and function. It is for this unity we
must ask God, since the churches are now suffering both
from the separations common to the world, which can be
resolved only in organic union, and from divisions related
to the manifold nature of the gift of the Spirit.

It is clear that the manifold gifts of the Spirit—the
utterance of wisdom, knowledge, healing, the working of
miracles, prophecy, tongues, discernment of spirits, administration, and the like (I Cor. 12:4–11, 27–31; Eph.
4:11–13)—are given to the Church and distributed and
appointed among all its members for the edification of
the Church and for service and witness to the world. The
charisms are the particular ministries exercised within the
total ministry of the Church. Not every member of the
Church has the same specific ministry. Nor does one member exercise all of the ministries (although St. Paul seems
to have had more than his share). Some of the charisms,
but not all of them, are associated with offices in the
Church, as with pastors or teachers, or with administrators
or leaders. But all of the varieties of ministries have their
place within the total ministry and within the unity of the
Church.

To observe the apostolic precedent of unity with respect
to the varieties of ministries broadens the meaning of
apostolic succession, an issue which remains such a stum-
bling block to unity and, specifically, to organic reunion
of the Church. Generally the term "apostolic succession"
refers to the unbroken succession and authority of the
ecclesiastical ministry, beginning with the Apostles, along
with the transmission of the apostolic teaching through

this succession. (As far as I can see, the transmission of the apostolic teaching is in itself a wholly sufficient—pragmatic, not doctrinal—reason for the institution of apostolic succession in the narrow sense.) In a broader sense, however, apostolic succession is something which pertains to the whole Church, and to all baptized people, embracing all the ministries of the Church and entrusting to every Christian the witness to the Gospel. It is this succession which is essential to the Church and which follows from the apostolic precedent of unity.

The ecclesiology and polity of the total community of the Church are not matters of indifference or unimportance, but they are secondary and auxiliary to the unity of the actual common life of the Church. The style of the common life of the Church and its members is most manifest in the sacraments given and ordained by Christ Himself: Baptism and Holy Communion. There can be no unity which is witness unless there be both a common understanding and universal recognition within the whole Church of the Baptism of each member of the Church. Nor can there be such unity unless all who are baptized are welcome into the common life of the Church, which is the Holy Communion.

Both Baptism and the Holy Communion are sacraments in the most ecumenical meaning of "ecumenical"—that is, both are sacraments of the unity of all mankind in Christ. It is perhaps misleading to speak of them as sacraments of the unity of the Church. They are that, but only in the sense in which the Church is called to be the image of the world in reconciliation. Baptism and the Communion—far from being esoteric, religious rituals—are most concretely political and social in character.

The Liturgy as a Political Event

Our gratitude for the contemporary friendly disposition among the multiplicity of people who call themselves Christians and among the several churches should tempt none to minimize either the profundity or the pathology of the estrangement to which all men who are baptized are heirs. These experiences of renewed contact, genuine humility, and mutual respect should not quiet the conscience of Christians but, rather, provoke greater awareness of continuing divisions.

At no point in the witness of the Church to the world is its integrity as a reconciled society more radical and more cogent than in the liturgy, the precedent and consummation of that service which the Church of Christ and the members of this Body render to the world. Of course, there are many Protestants who regard the liturgy as peripheral to the Christian life. Some even boast that *they* have no liturgical life, but this is a betrayal of ignorance, since liturgy means nothing more than style of life. In the broadest sense, all of life is liturgical. The conventions and ceremonies of courtship are a liturgy, articulating and dramatizing the love between a man and a woman. Or, to take a less attractive example—Joe Valachi, in the Senate hearing in which the chief witness expounded at great length upon the peculiar actions and symbols and rituals which constitute the extraordinarily sophisticated liturgical fabric of the Cosa Nostra.

As for the Church, all forms of its corporate life— from the Quakers sitting in silence in a circle, to the exuberance and patience of a Negro congregation, and the majesty and richness of the venerable Orthodox service—

are liturgical. The only serious question is whether or not a given liturgical practice has integrity in the Gospel. There are both laymen and clergy who regard liturgy as an essentially religious exercise—separate, disjoined, self-contained, unrelated—confined to the sanctuary and having nothing to do with this world. Some even regard liturgy superstitiously, as something having an intrinsic efficacy, as a means of procuring indulgences, as if God were so absurd—and so ungodly—as to be appeased by the redundant incantations of men.

There is, however, nothing so spooky or lucky about the liturgy, and nothing magical or mechanistic about its performance. The liturgy of the Gospel is, on the contrary, a dramatic form of the ethical witness of Christians in this world. In this sense, though there may be much variety in different times and cultures in regard to language, music, action, and movement, the liturgy is always charac-terized by certain definitive marks:

1) *Scriptural Integrity*—The liturgy of the Gospel is the theatricalization of the biblical saga of God's action in this world, thus relating the ubiquity of the Word of God in history to the consummation of the Word of God in Jesus Christ. A biblically authentic and historically rele-vant liturgy is always the celebration of the death and Resurrection of the Lord; the most decisive event in all history is remembered and memorialized in a context in which God's every action in this world since creation is recalled and rehearsed, and the hope of the world for the final reconciliation is recited and represented in the litur-gical portrait.

The scriptural integrity of the liturgy requires that the laity not be spectators but participants—not as a matter of piety, not merely for their own sake but because they gather, as a congregation, as delegates and, indeed, advocates of the world.

That is why the traditional Protestant "preaching service"—even when the preaching is an exposition of the Word of God, and not some religious diatribe—is an impoverished and inadequate liturgy for the Church; by the same token, that is why the Mass recited in the absence of a congregation, or celebrated in a language not familiar to the people, is a compromise of the scriptural integrity of the liturgy.

2) *The Historicity of the Liturgy*—The liturgy of the Gospel is both a transcendent event and a present event. It shatters the categories of time and space and location because it both recalls and dramatizes the estate of Creation in the Word of God, and beseeches and foretells the end of this history. As a transcendent event, the liturgy recollects *all* that has already happened in this world from the beginning of time, and prophesies *all* that is to come until the end of time.

But the liturgy is also a contemporary event, involving these particular persons gathered in this specific place in this peculiar way. The reconciliation celebrated in the liturgy is not only a reconciliation remembered from Creation or expected eschatologically but also in actual event the reconciliation here and now of those gathered as a congregation and society within and among themselves, and between each and all of them and the rest of the world.

That is precisely why the confessions and the intercessions of the people of the congregation within the context of the liturgy are so indispensable to its integrity. *This* is the time and *this* is the place and *this* is the way, in a most immediate sense, in which the whole, manifold, existential involvement of the members of Christ's Body in the everyday life of the world—both all that seems good and which men are tempted to honor or praise, and all that seems evil and which men are fond of rationalizing or denying—is offered and consecrated for the discretion of Christ Himself, the Redeemer of all men and all things.

Thus the liturgy is the normative and conclusive ethical commitment of the Christian people to the world. The liturgy is the epitome of the service which the Christian renders the world. All authentic witness in the name of Christ, exemplifying in the world the virtue of Christ, which Christians undertake in their dispersion in the practical life of the world, is portrayed in the liturgy celebrated in the gathered congregation.

3) *The Sacramental Authenticity of the Liturgy*—It is both this transcendence of time in time and the scriptural integrity of the liturgy of the Gospel which constitutes the sacramental essence of the liturgy. The actual, visible, present event retains all its own originality and contemporary significance as a particular reconciled community, and at the same time is transfigured to embody to the world the cosmic enormity of the reconciling accomplishment of Jesus Christ.

Thus the liturgy as sacrament is inherently different from religious ritualism, in which the propriety of the ritual practice itself is all that matters. (Such may be sufficient for initiation or elevation in the Masons or the Knights of Columbus, but ritualistic piety is radically inappropriate to the Eucharist.) Notice, too, that the liturgy as sacrament appropriates as its ingredient symbols, among others, the ordinary things of the common existence of the world—bread, wine, water, money, cloth, color, music, words, or whatever else is readily at hand. Sacramentally, we have in the liturgy a meal which is basically a real meal and which nourishes those who partake of it as a meal. At the same time, this meal portrays for the rest of the world an image of the Last Supper, of which Christ Himself was Host, and is also a foretaste of the eschatalogical banquet in which Christ is finally recognized as the Host of all men.

The liturgy, therefore, wherever it has substance in the Gospel, is a living, political event. The very example of salvation, it is the festival of life which foretells the fulfillment and maturity of all of life for all of time in *this* time. The liturgy *is* social action because it is the characteristic style of life for human beings in this world.

The Political Authority of Baptism

A particular confusion has arisen in the American churches, especially in this last decade, because of the clergy's involvement in direct social action. Although several Roman Catholic priests have lately been disciplined for speaking out on specific issues, this is a confusion which particularly afflicts Protestants, because they have far less certainty about the office of the clergy in relation to the ministry of the laity dispersed in the world.

What must never be lost sight of in the relations of clergy and laity is Baptism. All baptized people, whatever their work or rank, location or function, charismatic gifts or personal talents, share in the one ministry of the Body of Christ for the world *in* the world. Indeed, according to I Corinthians, every baptized person is beneficiary of the charismatic gift of faith. Baptism bestows the power to live in Christ as a servant of the world.

This gift and office of service to the world is vouchsafed

for all baptized people, and is not superseded or minimized by ordination. A clergyman remains, in a sense, a layman, and retains the same authority and responsibility as every other layman. Ordination gives him the office of priest and charges him with the functions of that office to serve the laity in the administration of the sacraments, the preaching of the Word of God in the congregation, and the nurture of the members òf the congregation, both as individuals and as a body.

It is, of course, often the practice to commission clergymen to perform other services in addition to those for which they are ordained, particularly in relation to the maintenance of the institution of the Church or the administration of a parish. These tasks are not essentially related to the peculiar work of the priesthood, though they may be essential to, or convenient for, the existence of the Church or of a particular parish. These are functions that a layman, however, might undertake, which means that priests, even in this parish, are sometimes engaged in work as laymen.

Ordination does not remove the clergy from the world, though that which characterizes their specific office in ordination is an esoteric and internal servanthood within the Church. Thus, clergy who become publicly involved in antiwar protests or in support of "my country, right or wrong," in the civil rights demonstrations and school boycotts, or as Kloods (chaplains) for the Ku Klux Klan and apologists for racism, or in public issues of any sort, do so as laity. There is nothing specific or peculiar pertaining to the functions for which they are ordained that authorizes such involvement. As with any Christian, what authorizes their political involvement is Baptism; what informs and disciplines their commitment must not be any personal whim or prejudice or any allegiance to worldly interests or factions but what it means to be a baptized person.

All Christians act politically and socially under the peril of dishonoring—and even, at times, disowning—the estate of reconciliation with all men vouchsafed to them in Baptism. Indeed, this fact is the Christian's only recourse against making political decisions according to the discriminations of other men.

For the man who is baptized, the world as it is, is precious. It is the recipient of love because God made it; as the Apostle James reminds us, His Word is to be beheld in all things and in all men. Christians are called to enjoy God's presence in the world for the sake of those in the world who cannot yet do so. While involved in this world, the Christian is characteristically, profoundly, and constantly immersed in the Bible, because it is the testimonial evidence of God's care for, and activity in, this world. From the Bible, we discern the manner of God's presence and vitality in the world's common life. Christians see the ministry of Jesus Christ as the example of what it is to be reconciled within one's self, with all men and all things in the mercy and judgment of God.

The Marks of Christian Involvement

In welcoming the Word of God in the world—and hence, in participating in the controversy and conflict of society—perhaps the first thing for both clergy and laity to keep in mind is that in this world there is no such thing as neutrality about any public issue. To be sure, some societies permit a greater freedom of involvement in public dialogue to their citizens and their institutions than do others, but in no society, least of all one which professes to be a political democracy, is abstinence from public controversy an alternative, or neutrality in public affairs an option. Every citizen and every institution is involved in one way or another, either by intention or by default.

Those who suppose they can withdraw only deceive themselves, because deliberate abstinence or asserted neutrality are themselves forms of involvement in politics. It is possible to conceive of circumstances where these forms of involvement may be intentional and rationalized, but let no citizen or institution, including the Church, be so naïve as to consider that these are anything else than particular ways of being involved in politics and social issues.

To take the most obvious example: In American society, the citizen who does not cast his vote gives the weight of his vote to the candidate who happens to win the election. His abstinence, or neutrality, amounts to support for the winner, since his vote, if cast, might have defeated the candidate who won. The issue, in such circumstances, is not really either abstention or neutrality but the uncritical and undiscriminating use of suffrage. Such a citizen allows others to determine by their votes the political consequences of his default. It is surely a form of involvement, but it seems generally a stupid way to be involved, except where there is no significant distinction between candidates—a circumstance which has often confronted Negro voters.

Much the same applies to the great institutional powers within a society. One has only to recall what happened in Germany in the thirties to see that what contributed more than perhaps anything else to the usurpation of political democracy and the rise of totalitarianism was the silence and default of Church and university. The Church and the university as institutions, as well as multitudes (though not all) church members and intellectuals, became accomplices of Hitler's rise to power by their blindness to political realities, by their preoccupation with academic theology, by their reluctance to speak out, by their refusal to protest.

There were, of course, the paramilitary groups, the radical anti-Semites, the political fanatics actively seeking to establish Nazism in power, but they were mightily and, in retrospect it seems, indispensably supported by withdrawal, neutrality, silence, and default by Christian people and by the intelligentsia, save for those few who did speak out and were either banished from the nation or imprisoned or condemned to die.

In politics, and most plainly in the politics of democracy, every citizen and every institution is involved, whether they want to be or not. Since this is so, the one virtually certain way to be conformed to the world as no Christian should, the way to be defiled in one's involvement, is in futilely practicing abstinence and supposing that one is thereby not involved.

The proximate and provisional nature of secular political movements and social issues in no way counsels Christians to be apathetic about such matters. Let it be as plain as it can be: although a deliberate abstinence may on occasion be rationalized, abstinence which is inadvertent or the fruit of apathy or complacent default or feigned noninvolvement is, theologically speaking, a form of nihilism, an affirmation of death as the ultimate reality in human existence.

For the Christian the necessity, and indeed inevitability, of involvement goes deeper than all this: the most elementary characterization of the Gospel of Jesus Christ is the Incarnation. The Incarnation is not a theological abstraction—though it is often presented that way in catechism. It is not some quaint or spooky figure of speech. It is not even a difficult mystery; on the contrary, the Incarantion means that God Himself, in Christ, has shattered for men the very mystery of His being and purpose and activity in this world. The Incarnation means that God's passion for the world's actual life—including its politics, along with all else—is such that He enters and acts in this world for himself. Apart from the Incarnation there is no meaning in the Christmas message that God is with men, nor in the Easter assurance that God acts in this world for the benefit of all men, nor in the Pentecost evidence that God inaugurates the true society which is the Church.

In other words, the Church and Christians are not simply involved in politics because of the nature of politics as such—by which all are involved and abstinence is a fiction—but because they honor and celebrate God's own presence and action in this world, because they know that the world—in all its strife and confusion, brokenness and travail—is the scene of God's work and the subject of God's love.

According to the Gospel, God is not confined to the sanctuaries of the Church. He is not enshrined in any altar. The reason Christians gather now and then in their sanctuaries is not because God is there but rather to celebrate and proclaim God's presence and action outside the sanctuaries in the common life of the world. Worship which has integrity in the Gospel is always an intercession by God's people for the cares and needs of the world, and always a thanksgiving—a eucharist—for God's love for the world. Worship at the altar is thus authenticated by the constant involvement of the people of the Church in the world's life and by the public witness of the Church in the world.

It is sometimes asserted that the Church should concern itself only occasionally in public affairs, where society is confronted with a "moral" issue. The problem with that view is that it oversimplifies the moral conflict in the world. There is no issue in society which is not a moral issue in both the transient human sense and also as one which God judges. In a fallen world, all men live at each other's expense, and every decision and action, even those which seem trivial or only private or unambiguous, is consequentially related to the lives of all men.

What you or I decide and do affects all other men, and every decision or action or omission is thus not only a moral but a theological issue, a sacrament of one's responsibility for and love for one's self and other men, or else a sign of one's disregard for and alienation from one's self and other men. Indeed, on the Last Day, though not before, God's own judgment of every act, word, and deed of every man will expose the true moral disposition of each man in relationship to all men. Meanwhile, each of us must make his own decisions, knowing that each decision is a moral decision with consequences for all other men, but not knowing what many of those consequences are or will be until he is judged by God's mercy. Meanwhile, each Christian, remembering his Baptism, must take his stand in the practical affairs of this world in fear and trembling.

But if there is no option of withdrawal, if silence is a form of involvement, if default abets the winning side, if all are in fact involved, how shall Christians and how shall the Church be responsible in their political involvement?

How shall they be involved and yet remain unstained by the world?

Surely the answer to that is: in the very manner of Christ's own ministry in this world.

There is no convenient set of rules, no simple blueprint, no simplistic ethics of decision for the Christian. The Christian witness in society does not consist of praising and practicing the "Golden Rule," which, after all, is a secular ethic of self-interest that demeans the essence of the Gospel. But there are at least some clues about the style of witness characteristic of the Christian life in the world, both for the Church as such and for the individual member of the Church.

1) *Realism*: The Christian is one who takes history very seriously. He regards the actual day-to-day existence of the world realistically, as a way of acknowledging and honoring God's own presence and action in the real world in which men live and fight and love and vote and work and die. And the Christian knows, more sensitively and sensibly than other men, that this world is a fallen world, not an evil world but the place in which death is militant and aggressive and at work in all things. The Christian knows that in this world in which, apart from God's work in all things, death is the only meaning, all relationships have been broken and all men suffer estrangement from one another and alienation from themselves. Of all men, the Christian is the most blunt and relentless realist. He is free to face the world as it is without flinching, without shock, without fear, without surprise, without embarrassment, without sentimentality, without guile or disguise. He is free to live in the world as it is.

2) *Inconsistency*: The Christian, in his fidelity to the Gospel in his witness in this world, will appear inconsistent

to others in public views and positions. He cannot be put into a neat pigeonhole, his stance and conduct are never easily predictable. The Christian is a nonideological person in politics, and there is no other label appropriate for him than Christian. He knows that no institution, no ideology, no nation, no form of government, no society, can heal the brokenness or prevail against the power of death. And though the Christian acts in this world and in particular circumstances in a society for this or that cause, though the Christian takes his stand and speaks out specifically, he does so not as the servant of some race or class or political system or ideology but as an expression of his freedom from just such idols.

3) *Radicalism*: That means, of course, that the posture of the Christian is inherently and consistently radical. (I do not use the word in any of its conventional economic or political connotations.) The Christian is perpetually in the position of complaining about the status quo, whatever it happens to be. His insight and experience of reconciliation in Christ are such that no estate in secular society can possibly correspond to, or much approximate, the true society of which he is a citizen in Christ.

He is—everywhere, in every society—an alien. He is always, in any society, in protest. Even when a cause which he has himself supported prevails, he will not be content but will be the first to complain against the "new" status quo.

To recall an example given earlier, many Christians at the present time in the United States are deeply and actively involved in the struggle to achieve integration in American public life. The Christian in that struggle, however, will characteristically be the first to recognize that integration of American society, as much as it is absolutely essential to the survival of this nation, is in no way to be confused with or identified with the Kingdom of God. Integration, from a Christian point of view, must be counted as a modest, conservative, attainable, and necessary social and political objective in this nation at this time. It is by no means the measure of reconciliation among men in this world.

4) *Intercession*: The Christian is concerned, politically, for all men in all the diversity of problems and issues of public life. Characteristically, the sign of the inclusiveness and extremity of the Christian's concern is represented and embodied in his specific care for those who, in a given time in society, are the least in that society, for those whom all the rest have ignored or forgotten or cast out or otherwise have abandoned to death.

The venerable ministry of Christians for the poor since the very days of the New Testament, for instance, is not simply compassion for their endurance of unemployment or hunger or cold or sickness or rejection by society, but is also, at the same time, a way of caring for all others in society who are not poor or who have some security from the assaults of poverty. The Christian knows that his passion for the world, his involvement in society, his stand in politics, his witness in the present age, encompass even his own enemy, even those whom he opposes in some specific controversy, even those who would deny the freedom of his witness, even those who hate him, and especially those who are threatened by his witness.

The Christian political witness, for the individual Christian and for the body of the Church, means demonstrating in and to the world what the true society is by the living example of the society of the Church.

The Christian political witness is affirming and loving the essential humanity of all in Christ in the midst of men's abdication of human life and despite the whole array of death's assaults against human life.

The Christian political witness is the audacity to trust that God's love for this world's existence is redeeming, so Christians are human beings free to live in this world by grace in all practical matters and decisions.

That is why the Church of Christ is the only society in this world worthily named great.